sto

FRIENDS
OF ASPL

S0-BRV-948

NEX

More Contemporary Americans

By Percy H. Boynton

810.4
B71m

The University of Chicago Press
Chicago · Illinois

BLACK GOLD

COPYRIGHT 1927 BY THE UNIVERSITY OF CHICAGO. COMPOSED AND
PRINTED AT THE UNIVERSITY OF CHICAGO PRESS, AUGUST, 1927

Foreword

Perhaps it is gratuitous—as being either needless or useless—to state that the following essays have a design and a central theme. It is stated most explicitly in the concluding chapter and the concluding pages—that in cultural matters the United States, the heirs to an aristocratic tradition, have grown away from their birthright and are in the midst of the experience of establishing a tradition of their own.

Of the four general essays the first and the last might possibly be interchanged; the two in the middle are attempts to mark two recent phases in the process of transition. The first group of specific criticisms are of men who wrote before their time, but whose recognition today is an evidence that the twentieth century is catching up with them. The latter three in markedly different ways are obviously spokesmen of the moment.

Acknowledgement is due to the "North American Review," the "Saturday Review," the "Virginia Quarterly Review," and the "English Journal" in whose pages various passages and chapters first appeared.

186185

Contents

CHAPTER I
Winds of Criticism

IT WAS an autumn evening in the late eighties. The Reverend George Hills was supping with his family on the remains from the collation prepared by the Sewing Society for the Wessex West Congregational Conference. Peace had reigned throughout the day. One or two orthodox youngsters had been ordained; the right hand of fellowship had been extended on installation of a new member from the North Conference, one from Hampshire East, and one all the way from Rhode Island. The moderator had sidetracked theological debate, only once resorting to a peremptory gavel; and in the Ladies' Auxiliary, an unlady-like discussion of woman's suffrage had been gently quelled by a complacent majority. It was an hour for ease and self-gratulation; but the reverend D.D. was so moodily silent that his wife had to know what the matter was, and having to know, asked. "I came over to the study this afternoon," he explained, "and I found that man Blinn nosing around among my books!"

What that man Blinn had been nosing around for was evidences of Darwin and Spencer and Drummond, which he would have used, if he had found them, not as subject of discussion but as grounds for proceedings against a preacher already suspected of heresy. Before long Mr. Hills, unheard and untried, was quietly shouldered out of his pulpit through the joint efforts of a plumber and a grocer who did not like to be disturbed during their Sunday-morning naps. This was shortly after Emily Dickinson had written a friend that her father brought home various books but did not care to have her read them for fear that they would joggle her mind; and not long after the friend, Thomas Wentworth Higginson, had described Lady Amberley as a radical because she believed in women's entering the professions. Eastern Massachusetts and New England and the United States, ecclesiastical and secular, were still what they had been when Emerson had commented on a people who assumed that divine revelation was ended, as if God were dead, and when Thoreau had deplored a ministry who could not bear all kinds of opinions.

The disinclination to talk things out which prevailed in these days is currently charged to the repressive influence of Puritanism, except by the champions of Puritanism who seem to feel that no sound defense can afford an iota of concession. There is no doubt that Puritanism left its blight of intolerance; all the major Cambridge and Concord heirs were free enough in lodging the indictment; all its theological survivors, who represent only the dregs of Puritanism, are freshly resurgent today. But quite as malign as intolerance was the narcotic influence of the Reconstruction Period. Post-bellum fatigue had lasted long and with all its normal effects. Fifteen years of exhaustion in which exploiters of every sort were the first to recover, confronted a still wearied respectability with scandalous conditions that they were too weary to attack. They were glad to be magnificently isolated from Europe's wars and Europe's woes, glad to be manifestly destined to millennial ends. They were compounded like Emerson of acquiescence and optimism and unmoved like Whitman to resist the meanness and agony by which they were surrounded.

There was even a veering away from conversation which might become uncomfortably provocative of thought. The old Boston Town and Gown Club was a thing of the past; so were the Radical Club and the Concord School of Philosophy which had survived in an unfriendly age to the amusement of a generation which battened on them for anecdotes. The Saturday Club itself was the arena for quip and jollity rather than good talk. Longfellow would not have been disturbed now as he had been in 1861 at the waste of an afternoon in the discussion of public affairs. Naturally in these days public audiences drifted altogether away from heckling. Speakers, even political speakers, were privileged; a challenger was hissed, or if persistent was hustled out as a disturber of the peace. When one day a pulpit favorite who conducted a gigantic Saturday Bible class was repeatedly interrupted he broke down and cried. If people who disagreed with him did not have the sense to stay away, they ought to have the manners to keep still or the self-consciousness to be humiliated at the first public rebuff.

If men and women actually spoke their minds they won no reply. What Emerson had said—he was now in Sleepy Hollow—was recalled as having come from Emerson. It was scriptural: inspired and authoritative, but sublimely irrelevant to daily life. Thoreau was an odd fish; young Lanier, a pretty poet. Edward Bellamy, with his utopian dream, could be comfortably discussed, for he said nothing explicit of existing human institutions or human nature. Howells, when he fell under the Tolstoyan influence, was still read as the gentle ironist of earlier repute. When the outspoken were not condoned or ignored they were contemptuously vilified: Whitman was an apostle of immorality; Bierce, the new man, a soured misanthrope. Mark Twain, seeing this, counted the cost of speaking his mind and decided it was too high. He knew that he might be ostracized, and he was certain he would not be adequately answered.

Even the liberals built neat and narrow walls each around his own little liberal tract. The Reverend George Hills belonged to the Twentieth Century Club, as a liberal should, but he felt slight respect for the heresies that were alien to his own. They were a choice set of cranks, he said of the membership. The crankiness of the English critics did not reach America. There was no general reading of Arnold, Ruskin, Pater. If people wanted essays they still turned to *Nile Notes of a Howadji*, *My Summer in a Garden*, *Reveries of a Bachelor*, and *Ponkapog Papers*. *Over the Teacups* sent them back to the "Breakfast Table Series" and farther back, via *Pen and Inklings* and *Bracebridge Hall* to the *Essays of Elia*. The current literature of the period was like the current domestic architecture and interior decoration. It was the day of Queen Anne exteriors and of miscellaneous ornament within. Current literature was employed to cover the ugly stuffiness of the furniture with doilies and lambrequins, and to embellish the corridors of life with edifying groups of domesticated statuettes.

Such an attitude toward life and literature is not hard to account for in nineteenth-century America. The whole people had long been under the uncomfortable necessity of facing a series of hard facts. Their forebears had started an ambitious experiment from a theory, and the later generations had done their best to develop a legend to fit it; yet the facts were out of harmony with both. Though England and Western Europe were similarly involved the renewing youth of the Old World was still buttressed by the experience of age. It was less hopeful than youthful America and less likely to be cast down by disappointment. But in the United States the democratic experiment was far from triumphant; popular education reduced illiteracy but did not perceptibly educate the populace. In the land of opportunity the rain fell equally on the unjust and the just. And all the harsh conclusions of this sort were given devastating significance through the growing suspicion that the Book of Genesis was no less of a legend than Weems's *Life of Washington*. Gone was the cherry tree, and toppling was the apple tree. For the overwhelming majority, whether Puritans or Transcendentalists, there was only one way out of the dilemma: Pippa's way. To the orthodox, for whom it was blasphemy to question the beneficence of any slightest providential dispensation, the only thing left was to shut their eyes as in that amazing piece of theological rationalizing, *Gates Ajar*. For the Transcendentalists the essential difference was the substitution of an ultimate optimism for an immediate optimism. By both the facts of the moment were to be discounted. "Everything is beneficent seen from the point of the intellect, or as truth. But all is sour if seen from experience. Details are melancholy; the plan is seemly and noble."

II

This was the state of mind of Mr. Hills's generation. The reverend gentleman himself was vaguely aware that he and his family had been caught up and buffeted by the winds of divers doctrines. As a practical matter he wanted to keep his feet on solid ground, but he did not want to think about the effort. He was lightly cynical about politics, voting the Republican ticket when he did not forget to, but he was reduced to speechless indignation when his eldest seceded to the ranks of Grover Cleveland, forgetting that a southern Presbyterian would have been just as shocked at the hatching of a Republican duckling in the family brood. His wife had proved that the pen was mightier than the broom and was paying two servants from a fraction of her editorial earnings, but she discouraged talk of equal suffrage and never thought in the abstract about economic independence for women. She had instructed her boys in the Shorter Catechism and helped send them to college. The boys themselves, returning as householders to a family week-end at the seaside, went in swimming under the subterfuge of taking a walk rather than disturb the maternal enjoyment of a churchless but unviolated Sunday.

The Hills family were solidly respectable America. Religion to them was moderately backslidden orthodoxy; the country, a vast residential tract; the nation, a metaphysical concept; higher education, a desirable predetermined program for youths who were not going into business; literature, improving entertainment; criticism, practically non-existent. There are many such families in America today, but not in the same stratum of intellectual life. The

Hillses belonged to the elect. Belonging to the elect they were on speaking terms with various tendencies: in the church, of course; in the market, as they were reflected in strikes, and tariff debates, and in the brief vogue of the publications known as Coin's Financial School; art meant painting and recalled Holmes's latest *mot* about Monet, on the same level with what he had written about Turner before the war; music meant the tolerant acknowledgement of Wagner who was a vagrant, like Weber, from the Olympus of Beethoven and the Pierian springs of Mozart and Handel and Haydn. And literature? Literature served to mark the immaculateness of an America uninfected by the contaminations of the Old World. Quite uninfected! Or at most, very slightly.

The Hills boys were brought up on *Sandford and Merton*, the Rollo books, and Miss Alcott (supplemented through their own enterprise by Henty and Jules Verne) and progressed to Scott, Dickens, and Stevenson. The elders read these latter and Stockton and Mrs. Phelps and Howells and Mrs. Ward and Mrs. Deland. There was talk of other books and authors: of Sarah Grand and Du Maurier, but their books were said to be tarnished and the Hillses instinctively veered away from them, and from Zola, and with less certainty, because of what Howells had said, from Tolstoi and his countrymen.

III

American complacency was not consciously national as yet. It was simply non-European; yet in time even this feeling became clearly enough de-marked to give grounds for the beginnings of a re-action. There were a few cosmopolitans in the coun-try who had all along been aware of the prevailing provincialism but had no leanings toward cultural evangelizing, and there was a normal insurgent group of young collegians, whose utterances were normally bumptious and biased, based as usual on enthusiasm and half-information. It was up with the *fleur-de-lys* or the shamrock or any other flower but the mayflower for them. It was art for art's sake and a-morality and triolets and pastels in prose; but most of all it was *Europa rediviva*. They were what young insurgents ought to be, and in the end they lent a fresh impulse to literary criticism and general criticism in America.

It was not because there had been no criticism at all in America that the enders-of-the-century could lead to a local renascence; it was simply because criticism resembles a play or a song or a picture in falling short of fulfilment until it is communicated, because criticism is not only like a quarrel but like almost everything else in life except suicide in tak-ing two to make it. Emerson had been canonized and entombed. Poe and Whitman, Howells and James, had written sometimes acutely, sometimes provocatively and without response. Norton, as his letters show, had kept ahead of Ruskin and had led him to revise many verdicts. Lowell, notably in "The Cathedral," had fallen short of the "Commemoration Ode" in eloquence but had excelled it in mature sagacity, though he was known for the "Fable" and "The Vision of Sir Launfal." Henry Adams was destined to wait for a posthumous *succès d'estime;* George E. Woodberry and W. C. Brownell, to deserve and to win the attention of a very select, very discriminating, and extremely limited clientèle. On the other hand there was Harry Thurston Peck.

Two critics have very recently supplied a nice antithesis in a pair of contrasting portraits—Mr. Sherman with a full length of Mr. Brownell, and Mr. Beer with a Kit Kat of Professor Peck. Mr. Brownell, potential mediator between the Party of Culture and the Party of Nature, is of course a distinguished representative of the former, but a critically understanding and tolerant one. His work, beginning with *French Traits* in 1889 and *French Art* in 1892, continued with *Victorian Prose Masters*, *American Prose Masters*, *Criticism*, and *Standards*, the latter four all after the turn of the century. Mr. Sherman doubted, with reason, whether any other critic in America was "more abundantly supplied with those general ideas in which the permanent value of critical writing largely resides," and whether any other has contributed as much toward "the definition of culture's own standards, the creation of a cultural ideal, the description of culture's business in a modern democracy." Mr. Brownell's first two books on the French character and its fruits in painting and sculpture belonged to an American period of awakening cosmopolitanism, and the chapters in which he brought his observations in France to bear on his own country were patriotic only in the painful incisiveness of their candor.

But Mr. Brownell did not write in the spirit of the discoverer or the exhorter. The culture of the Old World was not a new and exciting phenomenon for him and did not afford him grounds for the abandonment of critical standards. In fact, nothing was exciting to him and all he knew reinforced his faith in standards. Moreover, he relentlessly insisted upon thinking, and offered no resting places of biography, anecdote, gossip, or digression to those who would read as they ran. In this austere intellectuality Mr. Sherman found a defect not in Mr. Brownell's commodity but in what the brisk philistine world would call his salesmanship. So Mr. Sherman doubted, again with reason, "whether the art of criticism can, in the present state of our public, be most effectively practiced within the limits of this field," and whether such a practice does not very definitely limit the critic's powers of exerting an influence on a general audience. Mr. Sherman's doubt was a rhetorical doubt. He knew very well that Mr. Brownell's type of criticism will never directly reach a popular audience. But Mr. Brownell is doubtless uninterested in this fact. He writes in a passage not cited by Mr. Sherman that the end of a critic's effort "is a true estimate of the data encountered in that search for beauty which

from Plato to Keats has been virtually identified
with truth, and the highest service to criticism is to
secure that the true and the beautiful, and not the
ugly and the false, may in wider and wider circles
of appreciation be esteemed to be the good.''

This was not the message nor the manner to enlist wide attention in the days of *French Traits* and
French Art. It was an accepted gospel for those few
Americans of the generation of Arnold and Lowell
who read Lowell and Arnold. It was a gospel that
was deeply informed in the European culture that
was exciting the generation of Moody and Hovey.
But it was calmly aware of what it knew and uncal-
culated and unqualified to stir the group who were
throwing up their hats at Garland's *Crumbling Idols*.

Professor Harry Thurston Peck was more to their
taste, an evangelistic liberal preaching a miscellaneous doctrine of emancipation from everything
in general. Let us accept Mr. Beer's dicta, which are
set down in friendly admiration: He was a man of
"fractious brilliance," whose "interest in the world
about him expressed itself anyhow." "There was,
in the '90's, a distinguished but scattering and, of
course, ineffective effort toward a primary sophisti-
cation in American letters. . . . . Peck's importance
in the movement is clear." He and others "did what
they could, in varying ways, for the European continent in letters." One can imagine the gratitude of
the European thespians to the busy American call-
boy of Rimbaud, Laforgue, Vielé-Griffin, Mallarmé,

Krafft-Ebbing, Hugues Leroux, De Joux, Huys-
manns, Prevost, Sudermann, Hauptmann, and Remy
de Gourmont. One can understand why "a conventional female author of the period accused him of
taking unnecessary trouble in dragging out the foreign writers," and can harmonize this complaint
with Mr. Beer's own statement that "his mind was
a goldfish everlastingly drawn by some bright object to the glass of its tank."

And one dwells ruminatively on the paragraph
with which Mr. Beer follows this metaphor. For it
appears that the mind of the fractious genius was
continually "swirling off in fright to shelter in
weeds." Nietzsche startled him, Ingersoll scared
him, George Moore annoyed him. "He wanted to
be mundane, and . . . . honestly strove to be liberal," but he was beset by "the Puritan ghost." He
dallied with the thought of being an image-breaker
but was frightened by the work of the other icono-
clasts. He was a pathetically emancipated person
who was indeterminate and vacillating because in
his emancipation he found himself philosophically
without visible or invisible means of support. He
enjoyed at the moment a much wider hearing than
Mr. Brownell, but he has already become a fading
echo of a half-forgotten day.

IV

As between Mr. Brownell and Mr. Peck there
was no defined issue. As far as there was anything

fundamental in Mr. Peck's utterances, they were in
fundamental harmony with Mr. Brownell's in their
desire to enrich the culture of the New World with
the culture of the Old, and in their instinctive defer-
ence for the very standards which they were somewhat hectically challenging. In response, however,
to the journalistic vivacities of Mr. Peck the American reader indulged in one of his periodic rediscov-
eries of Europe, personally conducted by a number
of enthusiastic guides. One of the most spontaneous
and tireless was Mr. Huneker. In fact, Mr. Huneker
was the complete spokesman for his period—schooled
in music, versed in the pictorial and plastic arts,
theater-goer and play-reader, facile and energetic
writer. The number of subjects on which he could
speak with some degree of connoisseurship was impressive; the apparent extent of his reading was very
great. Yet his comments on the seven arts were always in the nature of specific evaluations, never in
the broad, and his allusive powers were limited to
specific artists and works of art. He impresses one
always as having had the cultural breadth requisite
for criticism, but of having gained it on the run and
of never having had time to meditate on what he
had seen and heard. He had his little audience, yet
after the eighteen nineties, and for a good many
years after, there was no critical expression in America that caused any measurable portion of the public
to stop, look, and listen. Mr. Woodberry? Yes. Mr.
More? Yes. Messrs. Mabie and Matthews? Yes.

But they gained no general attention, stimulated no new enthusiasm, challenged no preconceptions, defined no issues. They were the voices of a complacent period, so even toned that they evoked almost no interest and no reply at all.

It remained for the generation born in the last quarter of the eighteen hundreds and bred in the years bridging the centuries to begin talking in a new vein. By 1910 they became vocal. Whatever they had to say was reinforced by the events of 1914 and thereafter. An agitating decade had raised a hundred questions in their minds as to the meanings and values of all sorts of traditions, and the war was not a reassuring answer. They have united almost to a man in condemning the recent past. They have written in general approval of European culture. Puritanism, Victorianism, American provincialism have been their chief targets. Oddly they have never been concerned with the relation between European culture and European chaos, though they have been unremitting in their assault on the relation between American culture and American commercialism. The resulting controversy—since at last the day dawned of healthy controversy—has not been evenly balanced. The elders have scolded ineffectually or have kept silent, not being schooled in controversy and not caring to be tossed in a blanket or rolled in the mud; and the younger generation has supplied only a single really doughty opponent who did his best, though his temper and his tactics were unsettled by the noisy and contemptuous manhandling he suffered.

Whether their strictures have been sound or not, and certain of them are worth careful attention, the insurgents have achieved very real results in two directions. Mr. Mencken has sounded an alarum. Resembling Poe, the critic, at many points, he has paralleled him at none more closely than in the diabolical effectiveness with which he has trumpeted his cry to the fallen angels of democracy, "Awake! arise! or be forever fallen!" He has adopted the rôle of a western Bad Man and plays it consistently whenever he comes on the stage. He is no respecter, he hisses, of persons or of morals. The world is full of charlatans in the pulpit, in the classroom, in legislative halls, on the bench—everywhere. Diogenes was an idiot to waste his time on that famous hunt. The Bad Man would rather let blood than eat breakfast. He strides about the stage brandishing his silver-mounted six-shooters until the curtain falls to slow music. No one is ever fooled by the histrionic swashbuckling—least of all the actor. While the gallery is still thundering he lapses into gentle generosities, back-stage. But he wakes up his audience and sends them away all agog over his desperate villanies. It is an achievement of a kind.

In achieving this Mr. Mencken has contributed toward the building of that important property on the stage of life in which Mr. Van Wyck Brooks is

chiefly interested—a background of discussion. Mr.
Brooks has his own remarks to make about Puritanism, Victorianism, and American provincialism.
But unlike the Bad Man he is not chiefly interested
in shocking people. What he wants more than anything else is to persuade people to think. His quarrel with Puritanism is not because he hates it root
and branch; it is because it has been a mixed tradition and the negative elements in it have been at
war with those positive elements that are fine and
high. So what he aspires to is not so much to de-
molish an old faith as to proceed from Puritanism to
something better. To discover, he says, "the new
faith without which America cannot live . . . . to
build up that programme for the conservation of our
spiritual resources, is the task of American criticism." Thus in one way and another a critical interest has been aroused in young America, and a critical
objective has been defined.

V

As one reads current criticism one is led into a
distinction between "criticism in America" and
"American criticism." The first of the phrases is the
title of a book which is useful and illuminating because the essays collected in it so fairly represent the
main conflicting tendencies of the day. The only
tendencies they do not adequately represent are the
weaknesses of the more vociferous group; but these
protestants have fortunately atoned for the omission

with a volume of their own. The element of critical writing that might be qualified as in America rather than American is the element which limits its interest in literature to an interest in art, almost to the artistry of art, and which, when it concedes that human life is one of the prime subjects for art, limits its interest in life to the adventures of the human spirit regardless of the time and place of their occurrence or their recording. The spokesmen for this point of view are citizens of the world, or rather—in their identification of genius and taste—of that most sublimated of aristocracies which they are in the habit of calling the "republic of letters." They are the metaphysicians of criticism, and in the way of the metaphysician, however truly they may write, they write only for their fellows who like themselves are angels of one sort or another beating their wings in a luminous void. They have their place in the roster of the critics; and in their concept of the art of the critics they have much to bestow on the others who are inescapably interested in the life of the present. But the rarefication of their ideas and the detached abstractness of their utterances reduce them to faint overtones in the critical choir. If criticism as a work of art is like other works of art in being unfulfilled until it is communicated, these critics are not speaking with immediate effect.

No doubt the critics who are of the American world as well as in it are all concerned both with future possibilities and present conditions; but in point of emphasis they are markedly and sometimes violently in disagreement. They apply to themselves and to each other various tags and epithets which are more or less disingenuous; and, with certain rare and honorable exceptions, they incline in the heat of argument toward personalities which testify to nothing but the unpertinence of impertinence in debate. By and large they fall into two main groups: the critics who are chiefly occupied in showing how, from dubious beginnings, America has fallen into the lowest of low estates, and how the worst in American life and art is due to its culture and the best is a miraculous bloom from no known seed and with no perceivable promise; and the critics who are chiefly concerned with showing that there have been some virtues in the past and that there is some hope for the future provided the current corrupting tendencies can be checked and overcome.

The volume of essays called *Civilization in the United States* is a complete index to the mind and temper of the first group. Brought together by common interests and assumptions, the authors developed a desire "to contribute a definite and tangible piece of work toward the advance of intellectual life in America. We wished to speak the truth about American civilization as we saw it, in order to do our share in making a real civilization possible." In order to preserve unity and objectivity they decided to exclude from the list of contributors aliens, professional propagandists, and the merely disgruntled; the tone was to be good natured and the temper urbane. As determining the unity of the volume three major contentions prevail: "First, that in almost every branch of American life there is a sharp dichotomy between preaching and practice; we let not our right hand know what our left hand doeth. . . . . Second, that whatever else American civilization is, it is not Anglo-Saxon. . . . . Third, that the most moving and pathetic fact in the social life of America today is emotional and aesthetic starvation." If these contentions seem severe, says the editor, there is nothing to be said in reply except that the contributors attempted not to please but to understand clearly and clearly to expound.

Only the completely dispassionate and the completely uninformed can read the essays without some emotional response. Those who are predisposed to agree will thrill as to the anthology of a new set of Minor Prophets. The Hebrews from Hosea to Malachi are no more pungently outspoken than an equal number of the Americans. "We must change our hearts. For only so, unless through the humbling of calamity or scourge, can true art, and true religion, and true personality . . . . grow up in America." On the other hand, those who are predisposed to dissent will feel the stirrings of old resentments at the iteration of oft-repeated prejudices. They will read with renewed approval the charge from one of their own number that such talk is no more than a bid for notoriety. "I used to think that to insult the common sense, and always to speak contemptuously of the 'bourgeoisie' implied sycophancy, either to a corrupt and degenerate aristocracy, or to a peculiarly arrogant and atheistical lowest class. But our 'democratic young people,' as you call them, preserve and foster this artistic snobbishness as a form of self-expression." The uninformed should not read the book, for they will have no banks of fact between which to guide the spring flood of opinion. But to the dispassionate, who is willing to admit that these writers, many of whom he knows, are not unqualified fools or rogues—even though he is willing to admit their capacity for folly and roguishness—the book offers much to read and mark and something to learn and not a little inwardly to digest—if his digestion be strong enough.

On the whole he feels as he reads that the Minor Prophets are true to type.

> Who seem to carry branded on their foreheads
> "We are abstruse, but not quite so abstruse
> As possibly the good Lord may have wished";
> . . . . men who never quite confess
> That Washington was great;—the kind of men
> That everybody knows and always will,—
> Shrewd, critical, facetious . . . .
> And for the most part harmless, I'm afraid.

Put a group of Minor Prophets together in their youth, engage them in fortnightly meetings for a winter, set them to the task of speaking the truth about their country "without sentimentality and without fear," and let them resolve to declare themselves with good temper and urbanity, and you put them to a pretty rigorous test. However bold they may feel in the face of the public, they write in the fear of each other. What if the rest of the Prophets should charge one of them with being sentimental or cowardly? The thought is too awful. So they proceed sternly *fortiter in re*, and in order to be beyond reproach they admit no good of any American thing. But this part of the formula is easier of achievement than the other—*suaviter in modo;* it is far easier to select material than to adopt a manner, and urbanity is not the natural manner of the prophet. So while Amos and Obadiah, recruited from an outer circle, write in terms of natural geniality, the inner group fail in their desperate effort to be gay, as Haggai lapses into truculence and Habakkuk into specious levity. Yet these defects, whether in material or style, are after all defects of mannerism, and even though some of the lamenting refrains in the book become a bit wearisome when attempted by prophets who have not mastered the melodies and possess no sense of pitch, the insistence on the need of restudying the past in America and re-examining the present is altogether to the point.

This insistence, however, with a shift of emphasis, is just as vigorous in the speeches from the right wing. "By all means let us restudy the past," they say. "Suppose, while we are at it, that we study it in order to understand it, and not simply in order to flout it. And it is indeed high time to re-examine the present and to admonish it before it squanders all its heritage from the past." At this the left wing are noisily derisive. "*Gaudeamus, igitur*," they roar, the while they trample on the bones of their ancestors, "*juvenes dum sumus.*" To which the right wing respond with "*Dies irae.*"

To the dispassionate and innocent bystander like myself it seems as the conflict proceeds that more important than the matters on which the contestants are at odds are the matters on which they agree. As one who has sometimes been able to listen to dissent without a rising temperature, I question whether it is a *sine qua non*, as the most insistent conservative declared, to be a good hater. I concur with Mr. Sherman that the critic should have arrived at a philosophy of life, that he should know what he believes in, be able to explain why, and want to be convincing in his explanation. But Mr. Sherman maintained, and again I agree, that the finest product of civilization is a highly cultivated gentleman capable of playing a fine rôle with fine consistency. Yet this means that the critic, if he is to partake of the benefit of the culture he criticizes, must be not only a man of discrimination and conviction, but a man who plays fair and in courtly fashion. Dr. Johnson loved a good hater and was not unnaturally fond of himself. Dr. Johnson was a man of cogency and discrimination, but he was bad mannered and a poor sportsman. He was willing to misrepresent an opponent, to shout him down, to affront him into silence. His indulgence in hatred dulled his discernment till, in the manner of his kind, he drew no distinction between a good hatred and a petty dislike.

This is what hatred accomplishes, for, as Mr. Sherman said, it is the nature of it, like the nature of love, to dwell on one set of shaping thoughts to the exclusion of all others. Mr. Sherman hated the hatred of what he calls the "monoptic school of naturalistic critics and novelists" because of its unfairness as well as its unsoundness. He could see no good in Mr. Dreiser and say no good of Mr. Mencken; and he tarred his stick out of the same pot with his pet adversary. To either Mr. Mencken or Mr. Sherman the other has been like the posts along the walks that Dr. Johnson could never pass without tagging. When Mr. Mencken said "lascivious" and the other sneered back with "the young, the innocent, the inexperienced" one was uncomfortably reminded of the exchange of taunts between pugilists, the only purpose of which is to vent spleen and stir up the bad blood that resorts to slugging and hitting below the belt.

Aside from the matters of intense conviction which lead to the uncourtliness of recrimination, there is a set of differences as to the function of the critic which need not lead one into the tents of any camp, because, while they may be exclusive of each other, they are not inevitably hostile, and often seem clearly complementary. It appears to the non-partisan that a work of art justifies itself—if that is the proper verb, which he doubts—by its essential qualities and not by its conformity to canons of art. He believes that realism and naturalism have expressed themselves greatly at times, and no less so the various aspects of romanticism. He is no more disposed to champion one or the other of them as the climax of artistic endeavor than he is to champion the integrity of sunlight or attack the fallacy of shadows. He believes that it is as important for the critic to see and declare what the artist is trying to express as it is for him to discuss the modus of expression; that it is as important for him to reassert with the zest of the discoverer what is ancient and honorable in art as it is for the artist to discover the beauty that any might have seen and few have noted; that is, it is a difference only of approach and emphasis whether the critic seems chiefly to show "a heightened consciousness of deficiencies and corruptions in the scheme and distribution of values that obtain in any period" or to strive by positive precept to make reason and the will of God prevail. He knows, moreover, that most critics are specially gifted in some one of these directions, and that no critic can at any one time express himself in all of them.

If this be so, while for my own part I subscribe

with the critics who would contribute to a fuller, freer, richer American life—not yet despairing of the democratic experiment, and far from certain that I can look in any other direction for a larger measure of hope—even so I am unwilling to lose the stimulation of men of other minds. Since Mr. Brooks first uttered his wish that the winds of doctrine might waft America out from the Sargasso Sea in which it was foundering he has seen a partial but very definite fulfilment of his desire. In these latter years criticism in America has been doing its service to civilization in the United States, a service that could be performed only through the interplay of conflicting opinions. And now that many critics are vocal the finest promise lies in the fact that most of them are sure of the dignity of their undertaking. I have already cited certain of these. At this point at least the rest agree. Says Mr. Eliot, "Criticism is the . . . . development of sensibility . . . . and as sensibility is rare, unpopular and desirable, it is to be expected that the critic and the creative artist should frequently be the same person." Says Mr. Mencken, "The critic makes the work of art live for the spectator; he makes the spectator live for the work of art. Out of the process comes understanding, appreciation, intelligent enjoyment—and that is precisely what the artist tried to produce." And Mr. Spingarn goes a step farther in his contention that the critic as his highest achievement " gives us something that the artist as artist cannot give."

So criticism in America is implicitly an attempt by each critic to make of America the kind of country that he would like, which in every case is a better country than it is today. If the critic has had any real measure of experience he is certain that out of the past—his own, America's, mankind's—certain deductions may be drawn; and he knows too, if he have learned anything, that his own judgment is subject to error and that the worst errors of the past have been based on what was thought to be the ultimate truth. He becomes up to the level of his capacities an artist in his sensibilities and a philosopher in his procedure. As he achieves a sense of values he adopts them, and declares them, and tries to make them prevail; but all the time with the tolerance of the finite and the fallible manner of man he is. "And if he finds that he cannot succeed," as John Dewey, philosopher and critic, puts it, "that the attempt lands him in confusion, inconsistency and darkness, plunging others into discord and shutting them out from participation, rudimentary precepts instruct him to surrender his assurance as a delusion; and to revise his notions of the nature of nature until he makes them more adaptable to the concrete facts in which nature is embodied."

It is a longish distance back to that autumn evening in the eighties with the Hills family. One must leave the main-traveled roads of life and of thought to find the like today. The Reverend George was a

liberal who paid high for his convictions; his wife
was a pioneer. Yet one can hear what their comments would have been on these latter observations.
"Isn't that rather fine spun?" he would have said,
"Are that critic's legs long enough to reach the
ground?" And his wife would have been more direct: "Stuff! my dear. Downright nonsense. Let me
read you another chapter from *Rudder Grange*."

CHAPTER II
Herman Melville

IN THE equatorial seas, within sight of the desolation of the Encantadas, the isles of evil enchantment, looms the giant Rock Rodondo. It stands under unchanging skies, and through the surrounding circle looks out over the waste of waters. In one direction only, leagues away, the horizon line is broken by the lava heaps of the islands. They lie under a blasting sun in an unchanging clime, with no rain, no verdure, none but reptile life. On a time the buccaneers used a harbor there for the storing of their loot. Even they are gone. The rare sail that sights Rock Rodondo sights it and passes on. Lofty and alone it seems to have no part in life. Yet swimming myriads are in the surging waters about its base, and all up its terraced sides to the very peak are changing ranks of lighter and yet airier fowl, wheeling and screaming in the twilights of the day, and, when the sun is high, launched for far flights from above or stolidly perched on its lower stages. So Rock Rodondo stands, starkly enduring, in the midst of restless changelessness.

"If you seek," said Herman Melville, "to ascend Rock Rodondo, take the following prescription. Go three times round the world as a main-royal man of the tallest frigate that floats; then serve a year or two apprenticeship to the guides who conduct strangers up the Rock of Teneriffe; and as many more respectively to a rope-dancer, an Indian juggler and a chamois. This done, come and be rewarded by the view from our tower. How we got there we alone know. If we sought to tell others, what the wiser were they? Suffice it that here at the summit you and I stand. Does any balloonist, does the outlooking man in the moon, take a broader view of space? Much thus, one fancies, looks the universe from Milton's celestial battlements."

It was Melville's advice to those who wish to reach his solitude and share his view. When he wrote it he was looking back over a hard, short, varied struggle among men, and he was on the point of giving it up. Circumstance, even from boyhood, had always hemmed him in and frustrated him. In youth he had become so restive that he had shipped on a merchantman. The attempt to settle into village life after his return had been fruitless. Soon he had set off again, this time for years on a broken voyage to the South Seas, shipping on the whaler which became his Yale College and his Harvard. And always thereafter the spell of the sea had been upon him. It had given him story after story to tell, and it had given him a philosophy. Though he never returned to the sea he never escaped from it. The life of a landsman was a life of restraint. The tyranny of shipboard surpassed any tyranny on land, and yet the seafarer was free; for the sea was to him a symbol of the innumerable dreams and shadows and far excursions of the soul that are the lives and spirits of men. Like a surrounding mystery it encircled the world and was itself the deep and fathomless soul that includes nature and mankind. To a symbolist and mystic it gave "glimpses . . . . of that mortally intolerable truth, that all deep, earnest thinking is but the intrepid effort of the soul to keep the open independence of her sea; while the wildest winds of heaven and earth conspire to cast her on the treacherous, slavish shore."

II

Typee and *Omoo* were the first literary fruits of Melville's experiences on the high seas and on foreign soil. They form a continuous narrative. The escape from a luckless whaler and a tyrannical captain to the uplands of the island Taipi, the exposures and hardships of the first flight, the encounter with the natives and the fear of being converted into cannibal flesh, the idyllic life for months as guest and captive, and the sudden, thrilling escape fill the earlier and better of the two. The second records vicissitudes with a semi-mutinous crew on a worse ship than the former, a very much mitigated penal captivity ashore, a vagrant life and picturesque companionships among whites and Tahitians, and a third embarkation.

The books, and particularly *Typee*, are an extraordinary achievement for a man in the middle twenties. He seemed able without apparent effort to put character and action on the printed page, life and color so simply and so vividly presented that they have never been surpassed for these islands. Together the books offer a picture of South Sea life of a sort to allure the fancy of any victim of a driving northern civilization: soft climes and balmy airs, a relaxed and indolent people who have no need to be industrious, a whole male population who loaf and invite their souls, and women who have little to do but exercise their lovely graces. If ever natural conditions could permit such a life, it would be in this part of the world; and here the island folk, neither savage nor noble, peacefully idled away their lives.

Melville wished them nothing better, and because something much worse had been wished upon them by an invading race, he made his lovely narrative a vehicle for explosive information and opinion, foreshadowing what he was to do in increasing degree throughout his writing life. With his tongue in his cheek he compared the islanders with the *unco-guid* of Anglo-Saxondom. "In truth I regard the Typees as a back-slidden generation. They are sunk in religious sloth and require a spiritual revival. A long prosperity of bread-fruit and cocoa-nuts has rendered them remiss in the performance of their higher obligations. The wood-rot malady is spreading among the idols—the fruit upon their altars is becoming offensive—the temples themselves need rethatching—the tattooed clergy are altogether too light-hearted and lazy—and their flocks are going astray." It sounds as if Melville had just been rereading "Lycidas."

There was slight hope for the natives in the intervention of white sailors, consuls, and missionaries. These assisted zealously in the downfall of the decadent paganism. They usurped the best of the land and improved it visibly. The natives never cultivated anything deliberately—neither cocoa-nuts, bread-fruit, nor the vices of the civilized. So on the heels of evangelization there followed disease and premature death with a speed of depopulation that no warfare could rival. "Behold the glorious result! The abominations of Paganism have given way to the pure rites of Christian worship—the ignorant savage has been supplanted by the refined European! Look at Honolulu, the metropolis of the Sandwich Islands! A community of disinterested merchants, and devoted, self-exiled heralds of the Cross, located on the very spot that was defiled twenty years ago by the presence of idolatry. What a subject for an eloquent Bible-meeting orator! . . . . Nor until I visited Honolulu was I aware of the fact that the small remnant of the natives had been civilized into draught-horses and evangelized into beasts of burden."

Observations of this sort—and they recur a dozen times in the two books—could point in either of two interesting directions. They have carried readers into the discussion of the romanticism of the humanist as over against the romanticism of the naturalist, as they are likely to if one is inclined to the discriminations of the critic. But at the time among the representatives of church, trade, and the consular service they led to the question as to how much of a liar Melville was and to recriminations of the outraged that resulted in numerous elisions by the timid publisher of the second editions.

The young author seemed to document his missionary allegations, and it would have been quite out of his character if he had not, for he was a confirmed, and sometimes it seems incorrigible, expositor and documentarian. When the information was pertinent he introduced it with more or less of a show of pedantry. When it was unpertinent but suggested by association of ideas he introduced it too; and in both cases frequently at avoidable length. And, moreover, often when data were neither pertinent nor obviously suggested, but had only the most tenuous connection with what he was writing about, he introduced it with the zest of the born fact-monger. "Sadly discursive as I have already been, I must still further entreat the reader's patience, as I am about to string together, without any attempt at order, a few odds and ends of things not hitherto mentioned, but which are either curious in themselves, or peculiar to the Typees." Nothing could be franker; Melville never pretended.

"Not long ago," Melville wrote in January, 1849, "having published two narratives of voyages to the Pacific, which in many quarters were received with incredulity, the thought occurred to me of indeed writing a romance of Polynesian adventure, and publishing it as such; to see whether the fiction might not possibly be received for a verity." *Mardi* was the result. It is the work in which Melville, retaining all his feeling for the sea and the poetry thereof, passed over into the realm of allegory from which he was never to return. At generous length the opening narrative parallels the opening events in the early third of *Typee:* a seaman on a whaler endures the monotony of an unending voyage until at last he deserts. He survives the perils of the open ocean and comes to land. All this for a hundred and fifty pages is circumstantial and credible. 186185

But when he comes to land, it is land which never was, or rather it is an epitome of the known world. It is a vast archipelago, Mardi. As he enters the coast waters he encounters a boat with a priest and attendant worshipers taking to sacrifice a beautiful maiden, Yillah. He slays the priest and frees the maiden. She is Unattainable Beauty, and is soon lost, never to be regained. The remainder of the story is the quest, in which he is pursued by the avengers of the priest and continually lured by the messengers of Carnal Love, Hautia. The quest itself takes the form of a strange and fascinating Odyssey, made by a company of five: the hero, a king, a poet, a teller of old chronicles and quaint tales, and a garrulous philosopher. They course through the known world on a voyage equally unplanned by themselves and by the novelist. In its early stages it is a series of islands that represent types of living—the islands of the revelers, of the dreamers, of rogues, of gourmands, of the rich, the warlike, the island of litigation, the island of civil strife. Then the world ceases to be typified and becomes localized. The voyagers, ever seeking Yillah and nowhere finding her, go to familiar places: Porpheera, Europe with all its recognizable rival kingdoms; Dominora, England with the adjacent Kaleedoni and Verdanna; and farther away, Vivenza, or America. Yillah is in none of these, could not survive in any. Finally the voyagers come to Serenia, a consistently Christian land; but in their worldly wisdom they reject it as a manifestly impracticable community, and Taji, inexorable in his quest, goes on alone, though not until he has discovered that the attainable carnal love of Hautia is in no measure a compensation for the lost Yillah.

Melville does not refrain from offering now and again transparent reminders of what he is attempting to disclose:

"And pray, what may you be driving at?" interrupted Media.

"I am intent upon the essence of things; the mys-

tery that lieth beyond; the elements of the tear
which much laughter provoketh; that which is
beneath the seeming; the precious pearl within the
shaggy oyster; I probe the circle's center; I seek to
evolve the inscrutable."

"Meditate as much as you will," says the king
at another time, "but say little aloud, unless in a
merry and mythical way. Lay down the great
maxims of things, but let inferences take care of
themselves. Never be special; never, a partisan. In
safety, afar off, you may batter down a fortress; but
at your peril you essay to carry a single turret by
escalade."

Or, once more, "Now, then, Babbalanja," said
Media, "What have you come to in all this rhapsody? You everlastingly travel in a circle."

"And so does the sun in heaven, my lord; like me
it goes round, and gives light as it goes."

From *Mardi* to *White Jacket* was a natural step
for Melville, and it was taken very quickly. After
his first actual South Sea experiences, which readers
had refused to accept as fact, he made his return to
the United States on a frigate. *White Jacket* uses this
experience. Like *Typee* and *Omoo* it is based on fact;
like *Mardi* it is filled with allegory; and like the
coming *Moby Dick* it is cyclopedic in its information.
It is the chronicle of a voyage with no superimposed plot. The frigate "Neversink" becomes what
Mardi was, a microcosm of the world. The book is
compounded of meditation, myth, and maxim; but

(37)

at one point it disregards the admonition of Media and attempts with signal success "to carry a single turret by escalade." Melville's indictment of the practice of flogging seamen resulted in congressional action that ended it once for all.

There are fine characters and characterizations in the book. Jack Chase, first captain of the top, is a splendidly picturesque figure. There are thrilling episodes told with masterly skill; but through them all, now and then subordinated but never forgotten, the "one proper object" is pursued—to picture "the world in a man-of-war." And this world is freighted with passengers, who though fate ridden, are yet the possessors of free will. No man who had followed Melville's fortunes in the forecastle could be other than sobered and sophisticated. Yet, withal he came out from his years of duress with a simple, homely creed, orthodox in essence, and strong enough to withstand the withering influence of the grim world between keel and topmast. Fate rules impartially, but fate itself is controllable by mankind. "I have a voice that helps to shape eternity; and my volitions stir the orbits of the furthest suns. In two senses we are precisely what we worship. Ourselves are Fate." In this spirit he concludes *White Jacket:*

"Oh, shipmates and worldmates, all round! we the people suffer many abuses. Our gun-deck is full of complaints. In vain from Lieutenants do we appeal to the Captain; in vain—while on board our world-frigate—to the indefinite Navy Commissioners, so far out of sight aloft. Yet the worst of our evils we blindly inflict on ourselves; our officers cannot remove them, even if they would. From the last ills no being can save another; therein each man must be his own saviour. For the rest, whatever befall us, let us never train our murderous guns inboard; let us not mutiny with bloody pikes in our hands. Our Lord High Admiral will yet interpose; and though long ages should elapse and leave our wrongs unredressed, yet, shipmates and worldmates! let us never forget that

> "Whoever afflicts us and whatever surround,
> Life is a voyage that's homeward bound."

III

Typee was written, and *Omoo*, and *Redburn* the tale of his earliest voyage of all; beyond the chronicles of fact the romantic allegory, *Mardi*, great achievement, was written; *White Jacket* was written, and allegory was united with fact as well as with romance. But as yet Melville had not resorted to the richest of all his materials—whalers, whales, and whaling. In the order of things it was for him to turn next to this. "We that write and print," he wrote in a letter at the time, "have all our books predestinated—and as for me, I shall write such things as the Great Publisher of mankind ordained ages before he published the World." In such a mood he undertook the writing of *Moby Dick*.

"If by any possibility, there be any as yet undiscovered prime thing in me; if I shall ever deserve any real repute in that small but high hushed world which I might not be unreasonably ambitious of; if hereafter, I shall do anything that upon the whole, a man might rather have done than left undone; if, at my death, my executors, or more properly my creditors, find any precious MSS. in my desk, then here I prospectively ascribe all the honor to whaling; for a whale-ship was my Yale College and my Harvard." So he says in the midst, characteristically, of his greatest book. Beyond a doubt it was in this Odyssean college that he learned by analogy the way to proceed with his story: "There are some enterprises in which a careful disorderliness is the true method."

In the critic's experience of adventuring among masterpieces there can be only a few to equal the thrill of sailing the high seas with Captain Ahab. It has been said, and said again, that his pursuit of the great white whale is one of the momentous stories of all literature; but there are things that must be reiterated because of their imperative trueness. And this is one of them. Like most other colossal stories, *Moby Dick* has its offering to submit to every degree of literary acumen. On the surface it is the tale of Captain Ahab, long ago maimed in an encounter with the terror of the South Seas, of his consuming hatred for the monster, and of the voyage for revenge which ends in fatal conflict with the foe. Two-thirds of the chapters might be culled to present this relentless chase in the form of a so-called "boy's book." Yet even so presented the story would contain more than meets the eye.

However great it is as a literal whaling adventure—and there is nothing better of the sort in literature—it is greater as a story of life that is only incidentally told in terms of whales and whalers. This is the story of Eve and of Prometheus, the perennial story of man's struggle for spiritual victory in the midst of a world of harassing circumstance, and in the midst of a world where fate opposes the individual in the form of his own thwarting self. "All visible objects, man," says Captain Ahab desperately, "are but as pasteboard masks. But in each event—in the living act, the undoubted deed, there some unknown but still reasoning thing puts forth its features from behind the unreasoning mask. If man will strike, strike through the mask! How can the prisoner reach outside, except he thrust through the wall!" So Ahab maneuvers for the stroke, combats the world about him, seeks the unattainable revenge even as the voyagers in *Mardi* seek the unattainable happiness, and meets the fate of Eve and Prometheus and Beelzebub.

It is often said that *Moby Dick* is not an allegory. It is not merely a discoverable allegory, but in Melville's procedure it was as definitely and avowedly an allegory as *The Divine Comedy* or *Paradise Lost* or for that matter *Pilgrim's Progress* or *Gulliver's Travels* or *The Ancient Mariner*. As Ishmael embarked "the

great flood-gates of the wonder-world swung open."
As the ill-fated Ahab faced his doom he cried out,
"Pour ye now in, ye bold billows of my foregone
life!" And as the ship, staved in by the charging
whale, disappeared in the waves, like Satan, "she
would not sink to hell till she had dragged a living
part of heaven along with her."

Moby Dick is as didactic in its sustained and applied metaphors as in its carefully documented chapters on cetology, the lore of the whale. The ocean
is the boundless truth, the land is the threatening
reef of human error. The whiteness of the great
whale figures forth the ghostly mystery of infini-
tude. Human life is the product of the Loom of
Time, whereof the warp is necessity, the shuttle-
driven thread, free-will, and chance, the stroke of
the staff that drives the woof-thread to its horizon-
tal place. The whale itself is symbol of all property
and all privilege. Melville takes no chances at having these elements misunderstood or overlooked. He
expounds them at length and recurs to them in-
cessantly. If it be a sin to write prose allegory, never
man sinned as Melville. If it had been a sin, it would
have been a sin of splendor and not of bathos; but
as a matter of fact the only literary sinfulness in
writing allegory consists in writing bad allegory,
particularly if in so doing an otherwise good piece of
narrative is spoiled—as narrative is often spoiled in
purpose novels and problem novels, which are akin
to allegory.

Yet, regardless of the secondary purpose of *Moby Dick*, the story as a story is superbly successful. In spite of a thousand digressions the whole tale moves with a grim ruthlessness to its tragic outcome. Captain Ahab is more than an incarnate spirit of revenge. He is a terribly human being. He has none of the actuality of the fiction types in whom one may recognize contemptible or detestable acquaintances; but he is undeniably real with the reality of a Richard or an Oedipus. He pervades the ship with his unseen presence before he emerges on deck. He quells dissent with the irresistible power of a head wind at Cape Horn. He bends to his will those whom he cannot enlist in his cause. As the end comes near he is eager to joust with death. He carries the reader with him as he carries his crew; and leaves a vast silence behind him.

The book *Pierre* is an intriguing production and a chaotic one. Though it has a carefully devised plot and moves toward its tragic end with a relentless inevitability, it is not a good story, for it does not contain a single thoroughly human major character; and it is not a good allegory because it is not sufficiently detached from life, nor clearly enough superimposed upon it. It deals with the conflict between the claims of the conventional social order and the duties and claims of the individual. A young and wealthy aristocrat is adored by his mother and by a lovely and eligible girl to whom he is betrothed. Suddenly he becomes aware of the existence of an illegitimate sister, beautiful and poverty stricken. Without explaining fact or motive, in an evasive effort to protect his mother's pride, he wounds it to death by befriending the sister as her nominal husband. The mother dies after disinheriting him, and he lives out his last miserable days before suicide, with the sister for whom he now feels an overwhelming passion, and with the abandoned love who has now abandoned all to join the two outcasts in unhappy platonic devotion.

It is too much and too little to ask anyone to read. The characters are waxwork figures. They put Mme Tussaud's chamber of horrors to the blush. They are less convincing than hers because they are made to move and talk, ornately rhetorical talk with the strides and gestures of clumsy mechanisms. If the theme were overwhelmingly big, it might somehow overshadow the characters. But it is not. Pierre is a blundering and melodramatic ninny. His mother's alleged colossal pride is only a futile vanity. Pierre's first love is too stupid to see through him. His sister, though she is a duskily alluring beauty who serves often as the author's spokesman, is in the story no more than the occasion for the blunders and the futilities of the others. Yillah; unattainable beauty? Yes, but not the disheveled Isabel. Captain Ahab, incarnate hatred? Yes, he is a splendid madman; but Pierre is a quixotic lunatic. And yet one cannot climb Rock Rodondo or understand Melville without making *Pierre* a step in the ascent.

Melville at thirty-three was through with the life of the world and through with effective authorship. *Israel Potter* was to come, but it was a perfunctory piece of work not as interesting as the book it was based on. *Piazza Tales* were to come, pallid lotos-island reveries; *The Confidence Man*, an ineffectual pseudo-narrative treatise; and some metaphysical verses privately printed. But *Pierre* was Melville's last real and audible word, and even *Pierre* was an epilogue. He was done with story-telling or with the kind of criticism that is called "allegory." He was headed for a life of speculation in solitude; and *Pierre*, though to a degree autobiographical, had in it more of the future than of the past. He called the book in subtitle *The Ambiguities*. He wrote it in scorn of the conventional novels which were spinning intricate veils of mystery only to unravel and spool them neatly at the end, and in scorn of the compensation school of philosophy which held that clouds are provided solely for the making of rainbows. He was a skeptic as to the ways of the philistine world, more or less of an agnostic as to the detailed operations of Providence, but as much of a mystic in his ultimate optimism as the "compensationist" Emerson himself. He saw that "human life doth come from that which all men are agreed to call by the name of *God*, and that it partakes of the unravellable unscrutableness of God." "We live in nature very close to God." "From each successive world the demon principle is more and more dis-

lodged; he is the accursed clog from chaos. . . . .
Want and woe, with their accursed sire, the demon
principle, must back to chaos whence they came."

In another mood he wrote that for the enthusiastic youth there must surely come the time when
faith enters into conflict with fact, "and unless he
prove recreant, or unless he prove gullible, or unless
he can find the talismanic secret, to reconcile this
world with his own soul, then there is no peace for
him, no slightest truce for him in this life." The
talismanic secret, he went on to say, has never been
found, and in the nature of things never can be
found. Melville was neither recreant nor gullible.
There is little to tell whether he ever found peace.
But he disappeared from the life of men. He stopped
writing for the public, though he left behind, written at the end of his long silence, a last story of the
sea, *Billy Budd*, which was full of the sweep and
vigor of his greatest work, a final resurgence of his
energies not without parallel in the histories of
genius. But long before this he had set down in the
pages of *Pierre* the saddest of passages, which in the
light of all we know can be taken as a self-revela-
tion and a valedictory. It is part of a solid paragraph. I hope it is not an undue liberty to print it
thus:

I say, I cannot identify that thing which is called happiness;
That thing whose token is a laugh,
Or a smile,
Or a silent serenity on the lip . . . .

Nor do I feel a longing for it, as though I had never had it;
My spirit needs different food from happiness . . . .
For I think I have a suspicion of what it is.
I have suffered wretchedness,
But not because of the absence of happiness,
And without praying for happiness.

I pray for peace—
For motionlessness—
For the feeling of myself,
As of some plant, absorbing life without seeking it,
And existing without individual sensation.
I feel that there can be no perfect peace in individualness.
Therefore I hope one day to feel myself drunk up
Into the pervading spirit animating all things. . . . .

I feel I am an exile here.

IV

We are such sheep that because for a generation
there was no shepherd to lead us to Herman Melville, we passed him by. Bookish elders, gentle
readers of the old school, recalled him with vague
disapproval as the grandson of Holmes's "Last
Leaf," a renegade from the courtly traditions of the
old three-cornered hat, and the breeches, and all
that. He had gone to sea, not like a patriot, or a
merchant voyager, or a convalescent gentleman such
as young Dana, but as a South Sea vagabond. And
he had written things that were not for gentle readers, with none of the gentility that belonged to
Taylor and Stedman and Stoddard or even young

Dana, who all wrote of the faraway world as something to be contemplated in retrospect, or in the distance from an opera box or a club window.

Conscientious students and historians who wanted not to leave undone the things that ought to be done, dutifully mentioned the author of *Typee* and *Omoo*, but absolved themselves with paragraphs or half-pages. We gathered that the author was a good deal lower than the angels, lower than the antebellum trio, Cooper, Poe, and Hawthorne, lower than William Gilmore Simms, lower than young Dana—perhaps on a level with James Hall and Timothy Flint, to be reported as among those present in literary surveys to the extent of a paragraph or half-page. The publishers and booksellers, aided by a fire, ran out of *Omoo* and *Typee*, except for the few odd copies unloaded on the dealers in second-hand books. Of the tales that did survive any could be bought for a dollar or less.

Melville had poured his work out mainly in the ten years before *Leaves of Grass* appeared in 1855. The vogue of ornate romance was over with the decline of Byron and Scott and Bulwer, and the vogue of Dickens and Thackeray was on the increase. It was too late for Poe by the middle of the century when he died on that side street in Baltimore. The public could not be persuaded that life was a dream within a dream with the nightmare of the Civil War confronting them. And it was too early for Whitman, who regarded life as a very real succession of vivid, turbulent experiences and wrote about it in turbulent, vivid terms. It was no time for a man with the metaphysical inclinations of Poe and the superabundant vitality of Whitman.

What Melville thought about the literary predilections of his countrymen in the years before the war, he set down at a chapter's length in *Pierre*. They offered a drab and unpromising prospect. He accepted the situation, stopped writing for the public, bowed his head to circumstance and let it roll over him, and lived with his metaphysics in an almost total obscurity for the latter half of his life. When in 1891 people heard that Herman Melville had just died, they listened as to the distant echoes of an old melody, mused a moment, and forgot again.

But at last the inevitable happened. With the hundreth anniversary of his birth the reading public had been so awakened as to feel the wind of the spirit when it blew in the direction of Melville and Captain Ahab. Tradition had been so upset and trampled under in the years just past that a challenger of tradition and an inquirer into the ways of God and man found hearers. He had many rediscoverers. One, who read *Moby Dick* for the first time in late 1920, can be quoted for them all: "I hereby declare, being of sane intellect, that since letters began there never was such a book, and that the mind of man is not constructed so as to produce such another; that I put its author with Rabelais, Swift,

Shakespeare and other minor and disputable wor-
thies; and that I advise any adventurer of the soul
to go at once to the . . . . prolonged retreat neces-
sary for its deglutition."

So the pilgrimage was started to Rock Rodondo;
and every year brings more votaries.

CHAPTER III
Lafcadio Hearn

SOME of us whose memories reach back to *fin de siècle* days can recall from the nineties the occasional mention of a strange and exotic literary name and the recurrence of a new and mysterious political term. The name had the lilt of a fragment of verse, and the term insinuated itself into the consciousness of the elect with the quiet insistency of drifting leaves in autumn. We heard the name and the term over and over again with the uneasy suspicion that maybe there were people who knew what they meant, and that we ourselves might be able to learn if only we should try for a moment; but the suggestions in them were subtly remote, and the more urgent subjects of Kennan's Siberian exposures and the Dreyfus affair and the Boer War and the beef scandal drove them into the backgrounds of our minds where we were willing to let oblivion take the hindmost.

So we allowed them to drift by in print and dinner-table talk—Lafcadio Hearn and ''imperialism''— and we connected them in an association of ideas that was not altogether false, for both of them would have carried us beyond the confines of America if we had been ready to go; but most of us were unready. In matters literary and political we were anything but worldly then; we lived to ourselves, and at best we were neighborly and at worst bohemian. We oscillated between Old Chester and the Latin Quarter. As neither of them was concerned with imperialism we forgot about it; and we either forgot about Hearn or vaguely tried to fit him into the Latin Quarter, not realizing that he had moved away from all that sort of thing years before we had heard of him, and had become a citizen of the world who knew what imperialism was and had very little use for it.

A few people read his books and bought them—actually enough to bring him modest literary returns before his death. He was writing about Japan when we found him out. But we were interested in the new Japan that was whipping China and Russia, and he was writing about the old one; so the vogue did not spread very far. If we were to go to the Orient at all most of us wanted to see the Orient down to date, the Orient of open ports and cantonments, the tenuously bridged abyss between East and West, or the *opéra bouffe* Orient of Kipling. Yet some of Hearn's readers continued because they wanted really to understand some part of the Orient as seen by one who loved it. And others continued because they found that this observer had the soul

of a poet and wrote a beautiful prose. One little volume after another came out and had its little posthumous day, for the writer had died early in the
new century; until finally with a weariness for an
occidental world which had come to its logical climax in the great war, a larger public, who turned
away from daily circumstance with Hudson and
Conrad and O'Brien and Maugham and the rest,
have rediscovered Hearn as they have rediscovered
Melville, so that at last he has achieved the distinction of a mortuary monument in sixteen volumes
and a large paper edition.

If Hearn had not suffered so from his biographers
it would be intriguing to pose his case incognito to
a eugenist, a psychoanalyst, and a literary critic.
Specifications: an Irish father, surgeon in the British
army, and a Greek mother; loss of both parents in
early childhood; upbringing under the bony and
featherless wing of a prosperously Victorian great-
aunt; schooling in Roman Catholic seminaries; college in newspaper offices, first, in a transplanted New
England town on the banks of the Ohio, and then
in a gulf port where the last traditions of the Creoles
were waning before the up-and-coming makers of
the New South; at thirty-seven, three years of travel, or rather of foreign sojourn, mostly in the French
West Indies; and finally fourteen years of writing
and teaching in Japan, and death at the age of fifty-
four. Given these experiences to a little half-blind
and supersensitive man, what would Ireland, Greece,

the Middle West, the isles of tropic seas, and a Japan filled with invading aliens contribute to his culture? And what would his culture contribute to ours?

Yet psychological data are so elusive and their interpretation so debatable that it is better to remain on familiar ground. Literary amateurs in psychoanalysis seldom fail to be interesting if they have any gift with the pen, but they seldom succeed in carrying any conviction with them. They are too much like the zestful traveling man who has mastered the psychology of salesmanship in twenty lessons, and feels that all human life is compassable in a few pat phrases. On the other hand, the scientific gentry who can reduce art to the behavior of the optic nerve or the adrenal gland are usually so learned in nerves and glands that they have either misconceptions of art or no conception at all. Lafcadio Hearn long ago suffered much at the hands of one of these; and as if that were not enough, a new biographer, twenty years after Hearn's death, laboriously wrought together a fabric of purple patches in a spirit that was even more ghoulish than Gould's.

For the gossip-monger there is more or less to gloat over in the first two-thirds of Hearn's career; he can find a little here and there in the remainder. Hearn was undersized, homely, and near-sighted. The chronicler of his *American Days* harps on these facts with an insistence that approaches malignity.

In the early part of his literary career Hearn was at times morbid in his interests, and as a bohemian he passed through a succession of affairs with women. On these his biographer dilates with disgusting delight. Hearn was fickle, irritable, and sometimes ungrateful—facts which a prosecutor might introduce at the expense of a defendant, though they are critically irrelevant. Hearn was egregiously the artist, but his biographer seems not to have been interested in this. The hiatus between his artistry and his life was rather greater than in the case of Poe. Yet what Rufus Griswold did to befoul Poe is quite equaled by the inquiries and opinions of Messrs. Gould and Tinker. Seeing him with myopic eyes they lost sight of his mind and the depths of life and the heights of beauty that his mind's eye revealed.

Hearn was a romanticist who found his double impulse in a distrust of the theology under which he was brought up and the sordid life into which he was thrust, his philosophical support in the teachings of Herbert Spencer, and his release in a lifelong search for beauty.

II

His earliest memories of baby-boyhood were of being nightly condemned to the Child's Room, and of being locked there in the blackness—the light turned out for the sapient reason that the Child was afraid of the dark. Ghosts came and he was forbidden to talk about them, because they did not exist and could not hurt him. But as his benignant elders invoked the Holy Ghost he was impelled in due time to inquiries about God, and to hideous information about a malevolent deity who was chiefly the God of hell. The beauty of the surrounding world was obliterated for him.

Then came the revelation, through some finely illustrated books on art, of the splendid, virile, and lovely deities of Greek mythology. It was a thrilling delight—"the contrast between that immortal loveliness and the squalor of the saints and the patriarchs and the prophets" of his religious pictures—the contrast between heaven and hell. This fresh delight was soon assailed, however, when his pagan leanings were discovered and Christian propriety expurgated the pictures. The naiads, dryads, graces, and muses were rendered breastless, and modest garments were put on gods and cherubs—"large, baggy bathing drawers, woven with cross-strokes of a quill pen, so designed as to conceal all curves of beauty," with the result of affording the boy problems in restoring the hidden lines of grace. Finally, an honest confessional admission that he had desired the devil to come to him in the form of a beautiful woman was met with such dire admonitions that he was filled with joy at the hope that the temptation might actually be achievable. It was the final confirmation of his paganism; he never forgave Christianity. Not mature enough for speculative philosophy, he applied the pragmatic test, and was con-

tent to reject the religion on the authentically scriptural ground of judging it by such fruits as he could
know. Subsequent schooling in Roman Catholic
seminaries did not bring him back to the arms of
the church; and disowning by his rich relatives and
the poverty of his later boyhood failed to reconcile
him to the grimmest realities of a Christian civilization—the realities of the slum and the workhouse.
He had the solidest of grounds for his later "inclination to believe that Romanticism itself was engen-
dered by religious conservatism."

The revolt begun against dogma was reinflamed
by circumstances. From his late teens until his late
twenties he was living from hand to mouth as an
unknown. He suffered penury and hunger. It was
the kind of life that often drives men into crime; it
seldom keeps them immaculate from vice, for the
conventions are best conserved in conventional circumstances. During these years Hearn became acquainted with much that was horrible; and he wrote
about some of it. His celebrated report of the "Tan-
Yard Murder" revealed his powers, and shocked
some of his later critics. He had simply come to the
point of such emotional numbness that only a violent stimulus could stir him to utterance. For a
while he was a frank sensation-seeker. His steeple-
jack ascent of a church spire was in search for another thrill—and he got it and transmitted it to
paper. He described himself at the time as "the sensational reporter." "To produce qualms in the stom-

achs of other people," he wrote of himself, "affords him especial delight. To borrow the picturesque phraseology of Jean Paul Richter, his life path was ever running down into vaults and out over graves." But as an extremist, and an amusing one to his observing self, he believed not only in the "Revoltingly Horrible" but also in the "Excruciatingly Beautiful." In a little more serious mood he wrote to a friend ten years later, "I think a man must devote himself to one thing in order to succeed; so I have pledged me to the worship of the Odd, the Queer, the Strange, the Exotic, the Monstrous. It quite suits my temperament."

Yet before long he had come to a change of heart, possibly through the experience of feeling more certainty as to where the next meal was coming from and more stability as to his position among men. As "the sensational reporter" in Cincinnati he had liked to be shocking. It had been a lark to be bold and bad in print, and when he had been prevented, through rejection or expurgation, he had reveled in the luxury of persecution, for he had wanted to go the whole route with the French school of sensation. He might have known all the complacent joy of martyrdom—though his particular martyrdom was only muzzledom—if he had not somewhat suddenly become conscious of reviving Saxon inhibitions. He went over to the camp of the beautiful and was ready to out-Herod Herod in his abuse of the naturalists.

(58)

His reaction was no less violent than unpredictable. He protested at the "raw and bloody pessimism" of Zola, whose stories were a "putrid mass of realistic fiction . . . . literary fungi begotten of social rottenness." It all indicated to him an underlying national degeneracy. The French language encountered his wrath: it was peculiarly adapted to enshrouding the most awful forms of human depravity with exquisite art. The French masters were especially endowed for the deftest dissections in morbid anatomy. With the unction of a recent convert Hearn thanked his stars that literary conservatism still reigned in England and the United States. He was grateful for the prevailingly "brawny moral tone" that characterized Dickens and Thackeray; the power of self-control among English and American writers; the retention of the primal purpose of fiction, which was to re-create minds that were weary of the toil and strife of the world. The sensational reporter who had anticipated the *fin de siècle* decadents in pursuit of the horrible and the monstrous was become an ethical romanticist.

In this reaction against the world of Christian creed, the actual world of circumstance, and the artistic realm of naturalism and realism, Hearn continued to the end. In the life that surrounded him as a journalist he saw no more to admire in New York than in London, or in Cincinnati than in New York. Even in New Orleans the human city of the day was buried under a lava flood of sordid chicane.

The golden sunlight of eternal summer shone for him on a charnel-house of corruption. He was ready to abandon himself to cynical skepticism—was, in fact, abandoned to it—when he found himself under the spell of Herbert Spencer, thenceforth his literary superman.

III

The experience of Spencerolatry is a common one in literary history, but in Hearn's case it was an experience with a difference. Often the effect was to deprive the young believer of a comfortable faith. "The 'Data of Ethics' and 'First Principles,'" said Theodore Dreiser, for example, "nearly killed me, took away every shred of belief from me, showed me that I was a chemical atom in a whirl of unknown forces. . . . . I went into the depths and am not sure that I have ever got entirely out of them." But for Hearn, who was deep in the center of indifference, the effect was more like a positive redemption: "I . . . . learned what an absurd thing positive skepticism is. I also found unspeakable comfort in the sudden and, for me, eternal reopening of the Great Doubt which renders pessimism ridiculous, and teaches a new reverence for all forms of faith." In a word, what Hearn derived from Spencer was an approach to the study of human experience and a stimulus to pursue the study for himself.

The result of the study was a new artistic trinity of romanticism, idealism, and moralism. The mind, wearied by toil and strife, could be recreated only in escape from reality; the escape should be to an ideal world; but this was not pre-eminently a sensuously beautiful world, it was rather a morally beautiful world. As surely as there was a law of progress a new idealism must arise. The morals of the present world are avenues to the fulfilment of human possibilities. It is for this sound reason that the common sense of the mass always condemns any attempt to overthrow the moral code. Yet for the educated the new teaching of ethics should substitute a rational for an emotional morality, though it is fitting that for the mass the old emotional reactions toward the virtues should preserve the moral balance of the world. In the ideal world, however, this balance will be preserved through inherited instinct, and only in a social order where this prevails can the consciousness of the code be allowed to sleep. Short of this millennium, therefore, Hearn concluded, moral idealism must be sought and practiced because of its necessity as a regulating force.

In arriving at these conclusions, though he never strayed far from the trail blazed by his teacher, Hearn was not wholly preoccupied with following the marks. His eyes were open to the whole path and his imagination reached on to the end of the journey. So it developed that Spencer's dicta interested him not as finalities so much as reopenings of the Great Doubt. He saw what otherwise intelligent people are continually failing to see—that any doubt may lead the way to fine adventure, and that it is anything but a doubt that precludes all but one possibility. As a consequence, without clearly articulating his procedure, he moved on to the scientific theory of multiple hypotheses. He was already on guard against the Jack Horner type of philosophizing that leaps to fond conclusions derived from a single plum. He was willing to admit that to human vision truth is an iridescent thing, changing hues as the light plays upon it; that an old principle may turn out to be not quite true, and yet to contain an evident measure of truth that may not be rejected; that in the explanations of life an order of ideas, temporarily out of fashion, may come back into favor if it is found to offer a better explanation than the set which is in vogue.

Herbert Spencer might very likely have seemed to his new disciple an approach to infallibility even if Hearn had lived out his life in America; but the influence was doubled when Hearn found in the history of Japanese culture a multitude of confirmations for what Spencer had derived from other sources on the nature of individual and social life. His whole volume, *Japan: an Attempt at an Interpretation*, is interspersed with allusions to Spencer's generalizations and the corresponding facts in Japanese life. Near the beginning is the acknowledgment that "the evolutional history of ancestor worship, much the same in all countries, offers in the Japanese cult remarkable evidence of Herbert Spencer's exposition of the law of religious development." There are citations of Spencer in reference to the spirits of the dead, the longevity of religious dynasties, the intensity of patriotism in militant societies, the vague character of the Shinto hierarchy, the theory that the greater gods of a people represent the later forms of ancestor worship, even the thesis that elaborate pronominal distinctions prevail where subjection is extreme. The chapter on "The Higher Buddhism" is a running commentary on Spencerian doctrines, the book is appended with Spencer's advice to the Japanese nation on the proper policy toward occidental intruders, and the last reference to him in the text calls him "the wisest man in the world."

Hearn's sex philosophy, if it deserves so formal a name, was not unrelated to the Spencerian influence and was interwoven with his Japanese experience. It was not until he had attempted to think life through that his instinctive reactions became convictions and his convictions were translated into words. Until then his impulse seems to have led him to shroud in reticence every phase of sexual emotion or sexual experience. His reticence was not because the subject was holy, and not because it was base, but simply because it was intimately personal. It belonged to himself—though perhaps not quite as normally as the appetite for food and drink—but it was no more to be dwelt on than were the details of the digestive process.

Just this reticence he found in Japan; and as a teacher he found himself under the necessity of explaining to his students the depth and width of the difference between Eastern and Western thinking when he attempted to give them some understanding of the prevalence of love as a theme in English literature. "It is all very unfamiliar to you," he said in substance to them, "English literature is permeated with references to romantic love. You don't talk about such matters over here. You will be surprised, but you needn't be horrified. It is actually respectable enough, if only you understand it. You see, women in the occident. . . . ." To these boys he did not express himself as freely as to one of his old New Orleans friends: "We live in the murky atmosphere of desire in the West;—an erotic perfume emanates from all that artificial life of ours;—we keep the senses perpetually stimulated with a million ideas of the eternally feminine, and our very language reflects the strain. The Western civilization is using all its arts, its science, its philosophy in stimulating and exaggerating and exacerbating the thought of sex. . . . . It now seems, even to me, almost disgusting."

He inclined to be satisfied with the Japanese way of dispatching the problem by removing artificial obstacles. The social order belonged to the dominant male whose interests were divided between the worship of his ancestors and the perpetuation of his line. As there was no economic barrier to marriage he mated early, knew no suppressed desires, enjoyed the devoted subjection of his wife, and desired no intimacy of companionship, but held her in abiding respect as the lamp of the ever burning flame of life. Everything was done decently and in order—or at least if it was not so done, when the order was violated it was agreed not to complicate the social theory by acknowledging the violation. To the alien observer there were two notable exceptions to the code: the geisha, and the romantic love of folk and fairy tale. These were not even dismissed from the discussion. They were ignored; presumably as being unpertinent—obviously either too gross or too sublimated.

Yet withal Hearn felt that the golden mean was to be found somewhere between where he was and where he had been. There was something of himself in the Western life that he almost abhorred. There was something negatively unsatisfactory in the ruthlessly regulated life of the East. 'An overstimulated sense of sex "cultivates one's aesthetic faculty at the expense of all the rest. And yet—perhaps its working is divine behind all that veil of vulgarity and lustfulness. It is cultivating also, beyond any question, a capacity for tenderness the Orient knows nothing of."

As a good philosopher Hearn did not find in the romantic impulse any excuses for repudiating the obligations of life. His constancy to Spencer's leadership was equaled only by his constancy to his family; and they are of one piece. Deep in disgust with a surrounding world which in his latter years was choosing to blast him as "an atheist, a debauchee, a disreputable ex-reporter" he analyzed himself as Spencer might have: "My dear friend, the first necessity for success in life is to be a good animal. As an animal you don't work well at all. Furthermore you are out of harmony mentally and morally with the life of society; you represent broken-down tissues. There is some good in the ghostly part of you, but it would never have developed under comfortable circumstances. Hard knocks and intellectual starvation have brought your miserable little animula into some sort of shape. It will never have full opportunity to express itself, doubtless, but perhaps that is better. It might otherwise make too many mistakes; and it has not sufficient original force to move the sea of human mind to any storm of aspiration. Perhaps in some future state of. . . . ."

Here the voice of Spencer ceases and Hearn takes up the theme in his own person: "I think civilization is a fraud because I don't like the hopeless struggle. If I were very rich I should think perhaps quite differently—or, what would be still more rational, try not to think at all about it. . . . . I am already deemed the 'moral plague-spot' of Japan by the dear missionaries. Next week I'll try them with an article on 'The Abomination of Civilization!' . . . . But I have at home a little world of about eleven people, to whom I am Law and Light and Food. It is a very gentle world. It is only happy

when I am happy. If I even look tired, it is silent
and walks on tiptoe. It is a moral force. I dare not
fret about anything when I can help it—for others
would fret more. So I try to keep right."

IV

Throughout his career Hearn, the artist, was
pulled by rival forces. He wanted to prepare himself for writing and to write what would last. He
had had enough of making copy under pressure for
newspapers. At the same time he entertained none
of the illusions of the lazy-inspired. He must fill his
mind and plan his work and lay out ambitious programs and submit to the "Foul Fiend Routine."
And always he must keep his sensibilities alert and
wait patiently for the flash of perception that would
reveal a broad prospect or thrill him with the inevitable word. Nothing that could be known or felt
was inexpressible—but the right expression might
come—and for subtle feelings should come—as a
happy surprise. He must be an aeolian harp or a
sensitized plate, a medium prepared with slow so-
licitude to respond to the gentlest zephyr or the first
gleams of dawn.

His journalistic writing, to judge from the best
of it that has been recently reprinted, was facile and
fluent and obvious in its effects as such writing
should be. At that it was strikingly literary for the
columns of the daily press, even for the unyellowed
American press of the eighteen eighties. Hearn's

contributions passed from horrors to oddities and from oddities to fantasies. There was a measure of scrupulous translation from the French and an element of leaves from stranger literatures—Egyptian, Persian, Indian, Chinese, Finnish. There was a good deal of erudition in some of the papers. It sounds encyclopedic and some of it may have been drawn from thesauruses; but the titles in his own exotic library go far toward proving that he was a genuine delver in quaint lores. His liking for the recondite cropped out all through his career, sometimes as in the charming chronicle of Pere Labat, the Martinique pioneer, and sometimes as in the perfunctory literary and entomological summaries for which a Japanese student had done the preliminary drudgery. But the best of his writing, the part that is beyond chance of confusion with anyone else's, is the writing in which out of his vivid first-hand experience, or out of his delicately sympathetic interpretation, he preserves the evanescent charm of scenes and episodes and cultural traditions that are alien to Anglo-Saxondom.

From the time when Hearn went to New Orleans as an aged young man to the end of his short career his life was a succession of infatuations with places and peoples. In this aspect his romantic impulse was of the most elemental sort. The spirit of the quest was in it, but it sprang superficially from restlessness, the feeling that beyond the horizon was something fervently to be desired. The Creole life of the gulf port first stirred him as woodland and stream stirred the boy Wordsworth, needing no supplement unborrowed from the eye. Then the sensuous experience fulfilled itself as the dream became everyday reality, and he hungered for new scenes. If he went away, he said, to bleak climes, he could long for New Orleans again; but romance in one's grasp ceases to be romance. Or he could choose a less austere recourse and seek the sunlit life of unfamiliar places. It might be in Florida, the West Indies, Southern France. Somewhere else he must feel the thrill of fresh sensation. "Whenever I go down to the wharves, I look at the white-winged ships. O ye messengers, swift Hermae of Traffic, ghosts of the infinite ocean, whither will ye lead me?" And again, "If I could only become a consul at Bagdad, Algiers, Ispahan, Benares, Nippo, Bangkok, Nish-Binh—or any part of the world where ordinary Christians do not like to go! Here is the nook in which my romanticism still hides."

When the choice came, a ship bore him to Martinique, where the opulent exuberance of life enthralled him for a little. After the subtle reticences of the vanishing Creole tradition, this island of the West Indies confronted him like an extravagant whimsy of nature. There was an ostentation of wealth as of a *nouveau riche* among staid aristocrats; and an engaging naïveté. The silversmith's bracelets were displayed on his young wife's shapely brown arms, or around the chubby wrists of the baby who was car-

ried naked on his mother's hip. But the excess of
stimulant enfeebled his imagination; the color display numbed his senses; the myriad rush of new impressions dulled him to any single one of them; the
heat smothered him like a narcotic; concentration
was impossible. Yet a retreat to the farthest contrast from all this—a northern city—did not bring
the expected longing made articulate. In New York
there was no emotion recollected in tranquillity, because there could be no tranquillity for him in Baby-
lon. He was so filled with horror for the confusion
worse confounded that he had no room for happy
memories. He had written that he needed new vitality after two years in the tropics. He found it, and
with it a new and vitalized vocabulary: "I want to
get back among the monkeys and parrots, under a
violet sky among green peaks and an eternally lilac
and lukewarm sea—where clothing is superfluous
and reading too much of an exertion—where everybody sleeps fourteen hours out of the twenty-four.
This is frightful, nightmarish, devilish! Civilization is a hideous thing. Blessed is savagery! . . . .
I came in by one door as you went out the other.
Now there are cubic miles of cut granite and iron
fury between us. I shall at once find a hackman to
take me away. I am sorry not to see you—but since
you live in hell—what can I do?"

What he did eventually do was by a happy acci-
dent to go to another hemisphere. The nearest thing
to a haven of permanent refuge was offered him by

chance and accepted as confidingly as in the nursery formula of opening your mouth and shutting your eyes and getting something to make you wise. *Harper's Magazine* wanted "copy" on Japan and Japanese life that might serve as the vehicle for special illustrations. When Hearn landed across the Pacific he had reached Japan never to leave it, for he found there all the best that had intrigued him in New Orleans and Martinique: the fine manners of a seasoned culture filled with speechless dignities, loveliness of sky and sea and vegetation, freedom from the brute massiveness of occidental life. Added to these a temperate climate which neither sapped nor overstimulated, and topping all, a domestic life which, though it brought its happily acknowledged burdens, surrounded him with comfort and harmony and insured him peace of mind.

Once more, in Japan more slowly than in the West Indies or New Orleans, the first high fervor of enthusiasm waned. After the omnipotently beautiful splendor of the tropics the quiet gray-and-blue beauty of these gentler islands stilled and soothed him. The people were simple, charming, kindly; their games and their dances and their legends and their superstitions were immemorially old. Even when some of the inland villagers affronted him, they did it like harmless, naughty children. But all too soon he began to find out that in the gentleness of the people there was a baffling effacement of individuality; that the charm of all their half-lights and half-shadows was paid for at the cost of all brilliancy; that the immemorial customs had begotten an insuperable reticence; and that where there were no angers there were no hilarities—only the blue-and-gray levels of beautifully developed amenity and decorum.

At first Japanese life had seemed one with Japanese painting in their strange and curious and magical vividness, and he wondered why they both seemed so ghostly, until he discovered that it was because of the absence of shadows. Spiritually, too, they seemed to see life without shadows. "But not long ago," he wrote indignantly, "the West burst into their Bhuddist peace, and . . . . Japan learned how to see shadows in Nature, in life and in thought. . . . . Then Japan wondered at the shadows of machinery and chimneys and telegraph poles; and at the shadows of mines and factories, and the shadows in the hearts of those who worked there; and at the shadows of houses twenty stories high, and of hunger begging under them; and shadows of enormous charities that multiplied poverty; and shadows of social reforms that multiplied vice; and shadows of shams and hypocrisies and swallow-tail coats; and the shadow of a foreign God, said to have created man for the purpose of an auto-da-fe. Whereat Japan became rather more serious and refused to study any more silhouettes. Fortunately for the world she returned to her first matchless art; and fortunately for herself, returned to her own beauti-

ful faith. But some of the shadows still cling to her
life; and she cannot possibly get rid of them. Never
again can the world seem quite as beautiful as it did
before."

Nowhere in his sojournings had he found abundance of beauty and abundance of creative energy too.
Everywhere life was compounded of unequal values.
Under the most elementary of romantic impulses,
the mere impulse of restlessness, he had strayed
about the world, and with the larger impulse of the
life-quest he had hoped as he went, somewhere to
find force and beauty in balance. In his home in
Japan he seemed to have come to an anchorage; but
not for long. He must take his boy back to the West
for his education; if only to see Japan from a distance he must leave his family provided for and return for a while to the civilization he hated but
could not resist. He was buoyed by this prospect
when he died.

CHAPTER IV

Ambrose Bierce

AMBROSE BIERCE once wrote that literary criticism, which in any case seemed to him of slight contemporary value, was hopelessly obscured by the introduction of personal facts. His own reputation is not generally confounded by such material. Few know the story of his life; and the edition of his collected works contains no editorial comment about the man. In a section of one of his books subtitled *Bits of Autobiography*, and casually elsewhere throughout his pages, perhaps enough emerges—that he was a youthful northern combatant in the Civil War, that he was a journalist abroad, and at home from San Francisco to Washington; that like one of his own characters he succeeded in the last venture of his lifetime, when he "sought obscurity in the writing and publishing of books"; and that he finally disappeared without clue in the wilds of Central America in an oblivion from which his ghost is but now emerging.

His works can be found today on the shelves of many public libraries in California and in others here and there throughout the country, a definitive edition of a dozen volumes—the dozen library volumes that constitute the smallest respectable monument in the graveyard of literary dreams. They were published in 1911. They stand on the shelves undisturbed, their gray buckram only a little darkened, their gilt only a little tarnished, a dust smooch on the lower edges, a dust blanket on the tops, and the pages as unsoiled as when they came from the presses. They are seldom read, seldom drawn on for reprints. I take up the four collections of short stories within reach and find that the three avowedly American volumes are innocent of Bierce, the fourth including one tale of his among the thousand and more pages of best short stories of the world.

Yet the safe index of the price-mark shows that buyers of first editions are not ignoring his books— or at least not until they have bought them; the very bookish allude to him casually as to a neglected genius, though in a way that suggests a passing acquaintance with two or three titles and fifty pages of print; and now at last an occasional critic refers in detail to a definite work of his with the show of overflowing erudition that Poe, the critic, used sometimes to display. If Bierce were writing at present there would be a market for his products in the up-and-coming magazines. If his collected works had appeared ten years later they might have met with a welcome. But for any popular hearing Bierce

emerged on the American scene betwixt too early
and too late; though posthumously he seems to be
coming into a modest repute.

He was a voluminous writer, mostly in sardonic
observation on the life about him. He was born to
the manner of *The Devil's Dictionary*, a collection of
the caustic definitions which he composed during
the last quarter-century of his life. They are re-
stricted to human qualities and social terms and
define not what these are supposed to mean, but the
implications in the pharisees and hypocrites of the
dictionary. In publishing them he addressed them
to the "enlightened souls who prefer dry wines to
sweet, sense to sentiment, wit to humor, and clean
English to slang."

These same souls are the elected audience for his
Fantastic Fables, an Aesopian collection applied to a
nineteenth-century world of economics and politics,
and for the several volumes of his satirical verse,
mostly occasional. From these smaller units the
reader can follow along an ascending series of more
substantial and more explicit social criticisms:
"Kings of Beasts," designed in mere whimsy, but
rifted through with satire; "The Land Beyond the
Blow," eleven sketches after the manner of Swift;
"Two Administrations," prose and verse dialogues
attributed to members of the McKinley and Roosevelt cabinets; "Antepenultimata," essays on civilization, law, politics, religion, labor, and woman;
and finally "Ashes of the Beacon," the title essay

of the first collected volume, "a historical monograph written in 4930 . . . . on the lamentable failure of self-government in America," and "The Shadow on the Dial," the leading article in the eleventh volume, on the kindred but less desperate thesis that "our system of civilization, being the natural outgrowth of our moral and intellectual natures, is open to criticism and subject to revision."

Besides all this Bierce wrote the little, less than four volumes, that was the work of the artist who grasped rather than of the thinker who groped. *Bits of Autobiography* offers glimpses of life, unexpounded, at intervals over half-a-century, starting from wartimes when Bierce was "young and full of faith, /And other fads that youngsters cherish." *Can Such Things Be?* carries over into the realm of the supernatural. *In the Midst of Life* returns to the autobiographical background, and goes forward into the world of subjective experience where dwell all the fearsome creations of the mind. In this volume are the stories of Bierce that are read by the mythical "everybody" of polite bookdom: "A Horseman in the Sky" and "An Occurrence at Owl Creek Bridge." Topping all these is his one piece of sustained narrative, "The Monk and the Hangman's Daughter."

In both his journalism and his artistry Bierce was more nearly in tune with the nineteen twenties than with the eighteen nineties which chose to ignore him in his prime.

II

Bierce in his maturity wrote in a mood of conscious and dreary disillusionment. At rare moments he would permit himself a burst of wistful sentiment:

"Oh days when all the world was beautiful and strange; when unfamiliar constellations burned in the Southern midnights, and the mocking-bird poured out his heart in the moon-gilded magnolia; when there was something new under a new sun; will your fine, far memories never cease to lay contrasting pictures athwart the harsher features of the later world, accentuating the ugliness of the longer and tamer life? . . . . Ah, Youth, there is no such wizard as thou! Give me but one touch of thine artist hand upon the dull canvas of the Present; gild but for one moment the drear and somber scenes of today, and I will willingly surrender another life than the one that I should have thrown away at Shiloh!"

But for the most part he lived in the thought of his contempt for other people and their disapproval of him:

I dreamed, and in my dream came one who said,
"Because thou art all sullen, and because
Thou sayest thou hast not for thy country, love;
Because thou dost begrudge the foolish blood
That in the far, heroic days thou didst
(Or sayest thou didst) pour from thy riven vein
In testimony to thy patriot zeal;
Because thou seekest ever to promote
Distrust of the benign and wholesome rule

Of the Majority—God's Ministers;
Because thou hearest in the People's voice
Naught but the mandate of an idiot's will
Clamoring in the wilderness, but what
Or why it knowest not; because all this
And much besides is true, I come."

The whole democratic experiment, as he saw it, was dubious if not doomed. It was a scheme devised by "dupes of hope purveying to sons of greed," in which the theory of the rule of the majority was only an unrecognized disguise of the discredited formula that might makes right. In the United States it was a scheme saddled with an absurd trial-by-jury system with consequent criminal immunity for all women, corruption by predatory wealth which fostered a specious and malign insurance business, a murderous network of railways, and a high protective and highly provocative tariff, with an imminent and inevitable labor conflict. Nor could he see anything to be hoped for from the extension of suffrage to women, or from the organization of the workingman, for he could find no basis for any sound assumption as to the honesty and intelligence of the populace.

Naturally he believed that no statesmanship could develop in such a soil; politics was the rank weed to be expected from it. An elected officer assumed his duties in the face of a vote of non-confidence on the part of half, or perhaps more than half, of the electorate. He could not acquire political ex-

pertness because of the certainty of being soon un-
seated by someone no more fit than he. He stood for
nothing, since, said Bierce long before it was a current saying, the leading parties were indistinguish-
able except in name. The gullible "pol patriot,"
who resembled the pol parrot in his cast of mind and
"his deplorable habit of saying what you have got
tired of hearing," aggravated the case. The poli-
tician was willing to let the pol patriot handle the
tiller of state while he himself was working the
tiller of the soil; and he could listen without blush-
ing when the voter exclaimed,

> O statesman, what would you be at
> With torches, flags and bands?
> You make me first throw up my hat
> And then my hands.

Bierce had his early say, too, for the machinery of
justice, insisting on making the same distinction
between the law and the laws that he and many another before him made between the teachings of
Jesus and the ingenuities of the theologians. Again
and again he returned to the attack on the perver-
sions of law resultant from the intricacies of legal
procedure and the skill of legal experts trained in
the arts of evasion.

These untoward conditions on every side did not
arouse in Bierce the zest of the reformer. He was not
concerned lest one good custom, or a multitude of
bad customs, should corrupt the world. He was
pretty well convinced that the social order was be-

yond redemption. With the rest of his generation
he had quite evidently read his Darwin and his Herbert Spencer. He responded to the genetic findings
of the biologists with the pessimism that the first
encounter with science is likely for a while to stimulate in all active minds. Life was a harsh and hazard-
ous battle against overwhelming natural forces.
The reward was something neither to be relished
when gained nor missed when lost. And to cap all
as a forlorn compensation "we have set up fantastic
faiths of an aftertime in a better world from which
no confirming whisper has ever reached us across the
void. Heaven is a prophecy uttered by the lips of
despair, but Hell is an experience from analogy."

Yet beneath his negativism Bierce seemed to feel
misgivings about his misgivings—doubt of his
doubt. Spencer's omniscience was annoying, even
though his conclusions were not easy to gainsay:

> I know too well
> What Herbert Spencer, if he didn't tell
> (I know not if he did) yet might have told. . . . .

Bierce's invective against the laws carried with
them a subscription to the law as a body of agree-
ment about social behavior. And he believed ration-
ally in morality as a commendable and desirable set
of habits which the individual should establish in
himself. He was altogether scornful of the shibbo-
leth of a liberty which was set up in denial of social
obligation; and he abhorred the tyrannies of revolution equally with the tyrannies of despotism.

So he came round in the end, not at all surprisingly, to his "ultimate and determining test of right—'What in the circumstances would Jesus have done?'—the Jesus of the New Testament and not the Jesus of the commentators, theologians, priests and parsons." Bierce was not a Christian in any ecclesiastical sense, he was careful to explain, but he was a whole-hearted admirer of Jesus, who was pre-eminent to him as "a moral lightning calculator."

In the way of thoughtful doubters Bierce was out of tune with any set of extremists. To religious orthodoxy of the sort that associates doubt with vice, anarchy, and atheism, he was of course anathema, and quite ready to return objurgation for objurgation. To the a-moralist and apostle of liberty he was an old fogy because he still believed in a code, even though the code was to be derived from life and not imposed on it; and he could meet contempt with contempt. But unhappily he was of no particular comfort to himself; for unrelieved disillusionment hums a sad burden in a minor key.

III

Yet along the blind alley of circumstance, and above and around it, life still offered Bierce mystery and beauty. The mystery lay in the spirit world, in the indeterminable connection between that and the world of matter, and in the very marvels of intellectual and emotional happenings. The beauty lay in the chance of finding just the right words with which to narrate the adventures of the spirit.

In his best-known volume, *In the Midst of Life*, Bierce painted a series of pictures that are marvels of sheer vividness. Once read they are cut deep into the memory both by the vigor of the etching and the momentous significance they contribute to the stories that contain them. "An Occurrence at Owl Creek Bridge," although not above the level of Bierce's most effective writing, is most often cited because of its ingenious construction and its surprise ending: the discovery that the prolonged account of an escape by a condemned spy has been imagined in the moment between the drop of the hangman's trap and the fall to the end of the rope. Two days have brought every sort of vicissitude for a war fugitive; home, wife, and child have been reached—when the victim's body hangs lifeless from Owl Creek Bridge. "A Son of the Gods—a Study in the Present Tense" betrays in its subtitle Bierce's conscious enjoyment of a technique, as he develops in sharpest detail a long suspense passage leading to the splendid and inevitable death of a lone reconnoiterer watched by thousands of his fellow-soldiers.

The recurrent or constant factor in the book is extreme emotional tension. The characters are sometimes pathological and the situations abnormal. The people and the events they pass through are barely within the farthest reaches of credibility.

Bierce often turned naturally to war episodes, because, although actual, they were farthest from the even tenor of normal life. Even in these it was the rarest occurrence for him to reveal any sense of humankind in general. The mass, the herd, the crowd, was a dim background for one man living at the highest pitch and more often than not dying of the tension. And the individual himself was less a character than a piece of susceptibility played on by overwhelming emotions. So he writes of the unbalancing effect on a man of accepting and serving a term for burglary in order to protect his mistress from exposure; of a death following great expectations protracted for five years by the terms of an eccentric will; of madness induced by night solitude with a corpse, by isolation in the dark with what proves to be only a stuffed snake, by reading a ghost story "in suitable surroundings."

Bierce passes on to the farther edge of no-man's-land in *Can Such Things Be?*—a collection of stories in which he resorts to the horrors of the werewolf and malign specter as they appear and reappear in the Japanese redactions of Lafcadio Hearn. But between the products of the two men there is the obvious difference between the familiar and the exotic. Hearn's tales of shadowed offenses to visitants from the spirit land and the terrors of spectral revenge are matched by Bierce's use of occidental brute facts, the more horrible because of their daily recurrence in the newspapers. The attendant spirit of a loving wife is a possibility in *Kotto* or *Kwaidan*, but the murder of a loving wife under false suspicion of infidelity belongs to *Can Such Things Be?*—and so too, the tracks and footprints, the wild screams, the traces of struggle, and the mutilated remains of the bogies' victims. Bierce seems dedicated to the rousing of "pity and terror"—and then in the midst of the volume, the more conspicuous for the loneliness of its survival, is a little allegory called "Haiti the Shepherd" on the theme that "happiness may come if not sought, but looked for will never be seen," very pretty, very moralistic, very unlike its author.

Quite at the apex of Bierce's literary achievement is his longest piece of prose, "The Monk and the Hangman's Daughter," in which he most effectively combines his sense of beauty with his gift for subjective analysis. In a circumstantial Foreword he attributes the original to a German—who pretends to derive it from an old manuscript—and the first English version to a faithful but uninspired translator. His own version, he says, is a free rendition of this. It is a beautiful rendition of the story told by a young Franciscan monk of his hopeless devotion for an ostracized village maiden. She is lovely in body and spirit but an outcast because her father is the hangman and because she is suspected of being the mistress of the village gallant. The friar is repeatedly disciplined for defending her, and by slow degrees, told only in implications, he goes mad, and slays her in the name of the Lord to save her from

the lust of her admirer. He never admits to himself
his own lover's infatuation. He never realizes what
a postscript to the story reveals, "that the maiden
cherished a secret and forbidden love for him who
slew her in ignorance of her passion." The source
of the plot is a matter of small moment. In its present form the tale is an evidence of what Bierce could
achieve when he released his powers in pure artistry.

His gifts as an artist lay in altogether different and
conflicting powers. On the intellectual side he was
a sardonic wit and a humorist. The special endowment of the wit is based on a capacity for acute and
often acrid wording of nice discriminations. He sees
a discrepancy or an incongruity and brands it with
a phrase or a sentence. It is what Aesop did with his
potent "sour grapes" or what Sidney Smith did to
the suppressors of blasphemy when he said of one
offender that he was capable of speaking disrespect-
fully of the Equator. Wit imposes a sentence and offers a challenge. In the subject of wit there is little
to laugh at, though its turn of expression may pro-
voke a smile. It is directed at culprits who are both
fallible and responsible and therefore is always
turned on humankind. Though the high-hanging
grape and the oblivious Equator may figure in witty
observations they are never the objects of them.
What Bierce had to say in this vein is to be found in
the *Dictionary*, the *Fables*, and in a fair share of his
verses; and it was addressed consciously to those
who prefer wit to humor.

His humor was again intellectual and again in its casual play largely dependent on a gift of phrase. It emerges now and then in the more serious volumes, as in the passing comment on a nondescript building that it was "a somewhat dull looking edifice of the Early Comatose order, and appears to have been designed by an architect who shrank from publicity and although unable to conceal his work did what he could to ensure it against a second look." And in a consciously literary way it was frequently aimed at the specious and hifalutin styles of the fine-writing and eloquent-speaking schools. Throughout "Kings of Beasts," his gayest series, he fell foul of the dealers in rhetorical bromides, and often most happily, as in the passage on the muskrat:

"When he throws his eyes upon a tree the doom of that monarch primeval of the forest is sealed its caroar is at an end and the name a by word in the mouths of men, for he ganaws it down while you wait, and as it thunders to earth he raises the song of triump and lashes the air to foam. His house is fathoms five under the glad waters of the deep blue sea, and the steam boats pass above him as he pursues the evil tenor of his way, in maiden meditation fancy free."

In the fashion of Thackeray and Holmes and Bret Harte, Bierce tried his hand at parody, and he succeeded perhaps as well as they, which was only moderately well. For he was a satirist rather than a parodist; he quite lacked the flexibility of the latter. Nothing of this sort by Bierce can approach the best of Untermeyer or Carolyn Wells or J. T. Squire or the average of Max Beerbohm, whose *Christmas Garland* is the best of the genre since the *Rejected Addresses*. Always, whether as wit or humorist Bierce was taking the offensive against sentimentalism. On this ground he was more than a little suspicious of faith, hope, and charity. Feelings of any sort except distrust, scorn, and wrath seemed rather dangerous to him. The intellect must be a strong fortress against them all.

And yet sense was in the balance with sensibility, for Bierce was in the very nature of the case a man of feeling. So on the aesthetic side he added the delicate perceptions of the portrait painter to the caustic judgments of the cartoonist. The attitude and the utterance of the two are in complete contrast. The intellectual Bierce was always on the offensive; always ready to express himself in brilliant brevities. But the Bierce who wrote of the mysteries and the thrills of individual experience was receptive, deliberate, and deliberative, ready to surrender to a mood in a wise passiveness; willing to court in the shadows the shy thoughts that would not come out into the sunlight.

His shorter narratives inevitably suggest Poe, and can be comfortably laid on the Procrustes' bed erected by Poe in "The Philosophy of Composition." In scale, determination of effect, adoption of tone, establishment of background, and the rest of it, they submit to the same tests as "A Cask of Amontillado" and "The Fall of the House of Usher." But Bierce very properly resented the common report that he was a disciple of Poe. The tonal resemblance of their stories is clear, and it is clearly the result of their own resemblances in mind and temper; but in the most insistent feature of Bierce's workmanship, the elaboration of a single point of time for its subjective values, his stories are more imperatively suggestive of Victor Hugo's before him or of Stephen Crane's that were to come. One cannot read "The Red Badge of Courage" or "The Open Boat" without feeling that Crane may have learned a lesson or two—and learned them very well—from *Bits of Autobiography* and *In the Midst of Life*.

IV

The time when Bierce should have gained a hearing was between 1890 and 1910. His thinking, though not markedly original, was independent and aggressive and today seems somewhat provocative. He saw fairly straight when he looked at actual conditions, and he said very plainly what he saw. His printed resentment met with no general response. Much of what he had to say was implicit in Bellamy's *Looking Backward* which fascinated the multitude with an explicit picture of a communized Boston before communism had become a pariah in the public mind. It was rather more than suggested in

Howells' *A Traveler from Altruria* with its strictures on the ways of the fortunate and its flavor of sugar-coated socialism. But Bierce's methods were more direct and his opinions less hopeful. He did not believe in Arcadias or Utopias or Altrurias or Platonic republics. He rejected communism and socialism, and he was as devastating in his comminatory passages as the plain-spoken objectors in the Platonic *Dialogues* who are set up for the not always convincing rebuttals of Socrates.

But no one took the trouble to rebut Bierce. The reading public of these years was almost beyond the reach of the iconoclast. If it did not care for what a man saw it accused him of astigmatism, and if he foretold unpleasant things it called him a crank—not even a false prophet, which would have been a betrayal of mild interest. It did not bestir itself to analyze critical thinking; it was so much easier to dismiss all disturbing thought without analysis. It liked Lanier's prettiness without noticing that there were thorn-stemmed roses as well as lilies of the valley in the Lanier anthology. It contented itself with the nuances of Howells' humor and disposed of his Tolstoyan predilections as odd, but harmless. It considered *Looking Backward* to be an amusing fantasy. America was manifestly destined, and Pippa's blithe observation took care of the rest of the world.

> There was just a false note in the Tilbury tune—
> A note that able-bodied men might sound
> Hosannas on . . . .

while the devil took the hindmost. So Bierce said
his say on the ways of the world and the world ignored him—an exhorter at the gateway to Vanity
Fair.

It is not quite so easy to understand the almost
total ignoring of his prose narratives. The up-coming
of the *Yellow Book* and the *Chap Book*, Baudelaire's response to Poe and the decadents' discovery of Baudelaire, the vogue of Zola, the beginnings of an active
Russian influence, the emergence of Ibsen, Hauptmann, Sudermann, Shaw, the attention to the sterner voice of Hardy, might all have developed an
audience for Bierce. But they did not. Or it would
not be easy to understand if Mr. Beer had not recently reminded us that in the nineties the American
magazines, which were the natural channels for
American short stories, were charily discreet, print-
ing outspoken things that came from across the
Atlantic but rejecting and deleting from American
authors the circumstantial, the realistic, and the
grim. It was on this last account, he declares, that
Bierce's "Killed at Resaca" and "An Occurrence at
Owl Creek Bridge" were refused, and that almost
all of his stories might have been refused, if this
were accepted as due ground for refusal. So that
newspapers, literary supplements, and newly established weeklies were the refuge for sterner stuff if
the authors were alert enough to know about them;
and once printed in these, in the manner of refugees,
the grim tales disappeared from public view.

Ambrose Bierce

If Bierce were writing today he would have his audience. His social theses would not attract much attention—they are no longer startling—but they would be either condemned or approved. And the best of his narratives, equal in bulk to the best of Poe's, would be read, let us say, by the readers of Aldous Huxley and Arthur Machen, Sherwood Anderson, and Joseph Hergesheimer. For those who like good writing, whether it was done yesterday or last week, it is not yet too late to turn to the narratives of Ambrose Bierce.

CHAPTER V

The College Insurgents—A Bit of Genealogy

MAN'S feelings about the things that are nearest to him are usually more mixed than he will admit to himself, and always more so than he likes to confess to others. In public no one but an eccentric will confess to defects in his watch, his penknife, his family, his college, or his country. Off parade, if the facts justify it, anyone will curse his knife for a dull hoe, his watch for an old turnip. In the family circle—under provocation—he may say things that are too true for utterance. As a member of the opposition there is nothing too devastating for him to allege of the government. But on the subject of his college there seems to be no time or company when he will take a middle path between silence and rhapsody.

As an undergraduate I heard with horror of two Freshmen from Mercersville who confessed in the privacy of their study that they did not think that Mathers was such a heluva place. It seemed to me poetic justice that neither of them survived Sophomore year. In the decades since graduation I have heard only two alumni speak of Mathers in consistently disrespectful terms. One has gone the way of the dipsomaniac; the other sits in the seats of the mighty. Obviously neither is normal. Yet what I have seen and read in these last few years makes me want to talk about Mathers as I might among friends who are oh! so level headed and high above the quicksands of sentimentalism.

I

Speaking frankly in such company I would say that Mathers is a stately, odd, irrational, quite consistent, and fairly typical product of more than a century of American life. One might better say three centuries, because Mathers owes so much to its ancestry. It was a vocational school to begin with, though the founders did not call it so, not having invented the term, established like the old Harvard and the old Yale, by godly men to school young candidates toward the learned professions, primarily toward the ministry. The phrase they applied oftenest to the youths they hoped to ordain was "pious and indigent," with a hope for their piety and a certainty of their indigence if they were gathered into the fold. It was founded on the rock of Protestant orthodoxy, the tipping-rock of ages in which the protest is always disturbing the orthodoxy. And it was founded in the extraordinarily unstable decade when young America was uncertain of its experiment in democratic government, unsettled by its rapid economic development, and upset by the imported skepticisms of everyone from Goethe and Voltaire to Byron and Shelley and Tom Paine. "Republican" and "citizen" were the red political words of the hour; "unitarian" and "transcendental," the ecclesiastical terms of abuse by the old-guard. From mid-Colonial times Harvard had been falling back toward the heterodoxy that overtook it just before 1800; but though the seaport neighborhood of New England had followed the lead of Roger Williams, the Connecticut Valley had remained true to the Mathers and Jonathan Edwards. Very likely that explains why in 1837 Yale was the largest college in New England, Mathers was second, and the Harvard to which Emerson delivered his address on "The American Scholar" was third.

At any rate, Mathers was born of the old dissent of the Puritans, built by local enthusiasm, and established in orthodoxy. The undertaking was all very energetic and very human—a complex of hopes and prides and vanities and generosities and heart-burnings. As a result a little college was dedicated to the old faith; and dissent has been stoutly asserting itself there ever since. The vitality of the college was no doubt insured by the provident fact that it was not intrusted to an unchallenged despotism of saintliness. It was set up in a Yankee town of saints and sinners. If the theses of the Darwins were undreamed of, so were the faintest premonitions of the Eighteenth Amendment. Here was the new college with its slender enrolment, and across the road was the old applejack distillery with an annual output of no mean proportions. The farmers and the nearer neighbors turned out finely to erect the first building; and a furlong from where they erected it one of the townsmen not long after profiteered handsomely from a little acreage that the college needed to spread over.

The well-established American curriculum of those days, in its length and its narrowness, went back to the Middle Ages. The earliest hints of innovation were just being made. Harvard introduced the modern languages for the first time when Mathers Academy was flourishing. Jefferson developed at the University of Virginia a new theory of preparation for citizenship after the academy had become the college. And when Mathers became the college with the traditional aim of training preachers and pastors, it combined the traditional course of studies with excursions into these new fields, no less adventurous in proving to be excursions rather than permanent departures. The early work in the natural sciences was most notable, for this resulted in a distinction of teaching and an amassing of material at Mathers that was hardly even rivaled in America until Agassiz came over to make his great contribution to the culture of the New World. So the college which was dedicated to conservative ends was established on liberal lines. The issue was inevitable, though it was not yet defined.

The College Insurgents

For there were exciting times ahead. The actual charter was secured only at the cost of a long and heart-rending campaign. Pledged funds shrank, new subscriptions came hard, and the largest contributors perforce followed up their investments by heavy, if not reckless, underwriting. For a while agitation, both friendly and hostile, served as valuable publicity. Barnum could not have devised better. Students flocked in, and divinity seemed to be efficiently at work shaping the rough-hewn ends. But soon came a reaction. Some of the students, perhaps the less pious and indigent, had minds of their own; and regardless of the fact that cotton thread held the Union together, took up the antislavery cause. The college authorities tried in vain to cope with the situation, and, torn between principle and patronage, bungled badly. There followed repression and resurgence of free speech, a Preston Brooks episode in college chapel, an expulsion, and estrangement of southern support. At the same time a college issue of the day was raised on the troublous matter of commencement appointments, a Reign of Thorough ensued, the arch-rebel was made to eat his words—the original form of forcible feeding— and a threatened secession of the Junior Class was barely averted. It was an unhappy time, followed by an unhappy falling off in registration, an accumulating series of annual deficits, and the resignation of the second president with disaster impending.

At this distance the trouble seems to have resulted directly from blurred vision. President B, if his portrait is fair to him, looked like a vaguely bewildered Puritan. "The Puritans," Macaulay wrote, a year or so after President's B's inauguration, "were men whose minds had derived a peculiar character from the daily contemplation of superior beings and eternal interests." This much the look in President B's eye seems to affirm; but the peculiar character that Macaulay speaks of did not bewilder Cromwell and his followers, nor Roger Williams, nor the Mathers. It gave them a sense of eternal values that made them desperately practical in the world of affairs. President B, when he turned from the contemplation of eternal interests, seems to have been harassed by circumstances. Not being able to master them, he equivocated with them. All his utterances prove that he was fundamentally religious, but the fiscal history of his later administration shows that he totally lacked what Lowell called "eye-dollar-try." Or if he did look at a dollar, he became lost in the declaration of faith on it while the credit of the college was going to smash.

President C was a different manner of man. He had the face of Ralph Waldo Emerson, and the sagacity to see with Emerson that the scholar should keep his head in solitude only in order the more intelligently to ply his hands in society—that independence and sympathy were the best of housemates. Only a man of such a temper could have achieved what he did in the next nine years. It is an amazing story. When he took charge the college was insolvent. On paper it faced a staggering prospect of deficits. But the President and the faculty looked the deficits in the eye and stared them out of countenance. There could be no shortage of funds, they said, if there were no excess of expenditure. They could control the heaviest expenditure—their own salaries. They would pay all other bills first, and pay themselves out of what was left. At the end of the first year they divided among themselves the equivalent of one twentieth-century college president's salary. At the end of ten, the trustees moved that it was time to relieve the teaching force of a liability that had become an asset. The joint stock company—price of stock, one strong man per share —was now a prospering concern. And in the meanwhile the President had raised more money for endowment and buildings than had ever been dreamed of before.

At this point it is usual to sentimentalize over the heroic self-sacrifice of the men who saved the life of Mathers. For they were indeed heroic. But it is the essence of heroism that self-sacrifice does not enter into its calculations, that it springs from splendid recklessness, and is more engrossed with the things it hopes to win than in the things it is willing to risk. A minority of faint-hearts could have brought the whole enterprise to an ignoble conclusion; but the fighting spirit of the Ironsides was the one quick asset of the college when the pinch came. These men had the satisfaction of playing against big odds, of winning, and of coming through with whole skins. What made them win was something more dynamic than self-sacrifice, which after all is a negative virtue, though a virtue of which their wives and children may have been keenly aware.

II

There is another feature of President C's contribution to Mathers. He was a scholar, a pioneer scientist in the middle of the nineteenth century, and withal a staunchly orthodox churchman. The findings of science were coming into certain conflict with the literal interpretation of the scriptures, and opening the door to a series of speculations as to whether either human observation or human experience could rest content with the assumptions of a medieval theology. The conflict was soon to be launched, and Mathers was to be involved through its President. He had three courses open. He could go the full route with Emerson, and bid scholarship to be undeterred by established theology. "Yourself a newborn bard of the Holy Ghost, cast behind you all conformity, and acquaint yourself at first hand with Deity." But he did not go so far. Even at Harvard Emerson faced closed doors for nearly thirty years after he said this to the divinity-school students. As a second course President C could follow the steps of Jonathan Edwards, who turned away from his early and brilliant pursuit of natural science to become the last great champion of the tenets of Calvin. But this, too, was not for him. The only remaining course was to pick his way through the ambuscades of challenge which he faced in every field of scholarship, to find what reinforcement he could in human learning, and to repudiate or to ignore what he could not reconcile with his old beliefs. As between the divine inspiration of religion and the human pursuit of scholarship he was bound to assume that any apparent conflict should be ascribed to human error. And he so ascribed it.

In the account which President C gave of his administration he accorded due weight to the material gains of the college, citing them all as evidence of the grace of God. And in his mention of the students his whole emphasis was on their spiritual welfare rather than on their intellectual training. There had been some revivals before he took office, and there had been three thereafter. An average of twenty-five boys had been converted—one-seventh of the total registration. There was a type history for them all: a gradual preparation of interest rather normally developed; a period of electrical suspense and searchings of heart; and then a sudden precipitation of feeling which swept from the converted to the unconverted and enveloped all except the incorrigibly opposed, the emotionally inert, or the irretrievably frivolous. ("I might have entered the ministry," said Oliver Wendell Holmes, "if certain clergymen I knew had not looked and acted so much like undertakers.'') But the chronicles of these revivals reveal what they do not intend to emphasize, that there was a constant element in college that did not relish evangelistic stampeding. Some of this element seems to have been truculently irreligious and disorderly. One revival which had been hanging fire under President C was literally set off by a train of gunpowder when a preliminary meeting was in progress. At another time a group of recalcitrants, after heckling the regular worshipers for some days, held a series of meetings of their own at which they dared the faculty to convert them, and ended up with a succession of burlesques. But most significant were the cases of students who set their minds in respectful opposition and were finally brought round by revival methods to a complete and permanent change of view. After President C's day the revivals were less frequent, and in the eighties, when President E was in the chair, they seem to have come to an end.

This was in the natural course of events, for by the end of the fifth president's administration the declaration had been officially made for complete freedom of thought and inquiry. The fact was simply that President E, a transcendental philosopher, had eventually concurred with Emerson's contention that the American scholar should "not quit his belief that a popgun is a popgun though the ancient and honorable of the earth affirm it to be the

crack of doom." And as a further normal consequence Mathers partook of the history of its time
in progressing from the Puritan tradition, past the
phase of Victorian culture, with its emphasis on
character, to the study of the social order advocated
by Huxley and Ruskin and their contemporaries,
and thence to the modern enterprise of learning.

III

However, a historical appraisal of the period
which limits its findings only to presidential utterances and the educational abstractions of Milton and
Arnold and Huxley, who did not live in contact
with youth, fails to take account of the very vital
fact that throughout the terms of Presidents E and
F and G—from 1880 to 1910—the greatest impelling
influence in college life was inactive: the energizing
power of a positive set of convictions prevalent in
the student body. For the first fifty years this had
been an active religious influence. A large proportion of the entering students had accepted the Christian faith before coming to college. For several decades no student had passed through his four years
without experiencing a revival. At these times the
converted prayed for and labored with the unregen-
erate. Of the first two thousand who graduated almost half became ministers or missionaries. In all
these years it was impossible for a boy to go through
college without facing the issue of accepting or rejecting the Christian faith.

Then in face of the disquieting doubts which prevailed in the latter part of the nineteenth century, the active forces in behalf of orthodoxy began to lose ground. The college presidents and the faculties remained steadfast in the old faith, but the college bodies, subject then as always to novel and negative currents, drifted into a center of indifference. A powerful unifying and motivating force in student life had waned. "The coarseness and rudeness of action, speech and fibre which disgraced many a well-meaning student," recalled by Professor T, encountered fewer lets and hindrances than in the days that had gone before. When his question was put, "If we could not feel in our minds and hearts [as they evidently did not] the beauty of the Classics, the dignity of Mathematics, the glory of divine Philosophy, what could Heaven signify to us?" there was a steadily increasing number for whom the rhetorical question had no cogency; who were ready to reply, undisturbed, "What, after all, *does* Heaven signify?"

In such circumstances, teachers, however great, labored against odds that were even greater. Here and there a man stood out for years in spite of everything; but the strongest of the old professors fought losing battles, and many men of distinction secured only an occasional response from exceptional students in whom no rising disregard for the things that are more excellent could quench the intellectual spark. Thus it befell that by the eighteen nineties the old religious zeal had departed, no new enthusiasm stronger than the college spirit that rallies round athletic teams had come to replace it, and Mathers had developed into a pleasant four-year haven of refuge for the not-too-energetic. It was the transitional time from the vocational college to the vacational college; and Mathers was by no means the sole example of its kind.

It is well within the memory of honest middle-age that in the nineties a youth could go to an eastern college from a conservative home, open in a normal degree to group influences, and could come through and away unaffected in any vital fashion. No group within his line of vision was intensely interested in anything. No element in his class was actively conscious of the values or the purposes of education. An occasional solitary with such a point of view was generously tolerated as a freak. Certain boys mastered their assignments competently and in turn were assigned college honors. Yet to study obviously was to be a "greasy grind"; to fraternize with any of the faculty was to be a "leg-puller." Some of the boys were lazily faithful to the rites of the church, even to the extent of maintaining perfunctory class prayer-meetings. The ribald and the vicious showed the highest degree of infectious individualism, but were disappointing to a well-bred youth because of the frequent badness of their manners and the usual vulgarity of their talk. Conventional correctness and a certain timidity might keep him safely within the bounds of good conduct, but he seldom found his habits reinforced by positive religious or ethical convictions. Such a boy could secure a *cum laude* in the nineties, learning his lessons, unallured by facts, uninoculated with any ideas, the influence of the pre-eminent teachers offset by the almost universal student indifference, and he could set his face toward his "work in the world," in honest doubt as to whether he was capable of any honest study.

The fault did not lie with the colleges. It lay with the nineties. The phrase of the day for everything decadent was *fin de siècle*. The period recalls the Siberian exposures, and the Dreyfus trials and the Boer War and the rise of Mark Hanna. The slight tillation over *Robert Elsmere* and *Looking Backward* was past. It was no longer possible to stimulate a respectable excitement even anent a heresy trial. Within a five-year period had occurred the deaths of Browning, Tennyson, Arnold, Ruskin, Morris, Holmes, Lowell, Whittier, and Whitman. There were no apparent successors in the English-speaking world, and the greater voices from Scandinavia, Germany, and Russia were not yet audible on this side the Atlantic. Kipling was the literary idol of the day. The *Yellow Book* and the *Chap Book* and all their progeny contributed triolets, villanelles, rondels, rondeaus, and pastels in prose. At this distance we can see that there were signs of new life, but at close range if any had the vision to see them, few were bold enough to herald them, and those few were ignored. It was a lackadaisical time. Tiddledy-Winks and Pigs in Clover!

Then came the Spanish War. But that three months' excitement was not prolonged enough to waken the country, which was soon somnolent again, magnificently isolated and manifestly destined, with no acknowledged responsibility on the shoulders of the respectable citizen. Thus, as far as popular consciousness was concerned, matters hung till 1914; and thus they hung, too, as far as Mathers and the colleges of its type were concerned.

Mathers was oblivious of the development of the women's colleges which had sprung up during its later years. It was for the most part unregardful of the state universities, of which it had little conception, thinking of them as philistine vocational schools rather than as gigantic colleges. Among the vocational schools it favored the agricultural colleges with tolerance now instead of with the scorn of former days. And it stood as a complacent pharisee against the tendencies of every kind of school of technology. But while it subscribed in word to the traditions of a classical curriculum as "the parent of improvement, progress, conservatism," by a fine *non sequitur* of its own professions it followed the current of the times in paying unprecedented attention to the social sciences, the study of which was charged in one alumni manifesto as being "one of the causes of the increasing excitability of Ameri-

can politics." Thus the spirit of the times was at
work.

And now, in the last dozen years there has come
a renascence of student interest in the colleges,
which is bringing to the enterprise of learning the
zest that used to belong to the enterprise of religion;
and in this reawakening Mathers is no more unique
than it was in the sleep of the nineties. Throughout
the student world, in varying but perceptible degrees, can be seen once more the energizing power of
a positive and prevalent attitude of mind.

IV

Two obvious influences were at work to effect a
startling mutation of species from the grandfathers
and the fathers to the college boy of today. One was
the changed attitude toward the child; the other,
the World War.

The fathers were brought up under certain prevailing assumptions about childhood. "Little pitchers have big ears"; "Children should be seen and not
heard." When the grandfather reluctantly took
down the ruler, he thought to himself, "Spare the
ruler and spoil the unruly," and when the grand-
mother buttoned up the black-velvet Sunday suit
with the lace collar, she said, "Mind your p's and
q's," explaining, if asked, that the initials stood for
"polites" and "quiets." And these general assumptions, which were counterbalanced in the home by
all the human and humane acts of kindness and of

love that belong to family life, were dominant in the school where there was little or nothing to offset them. Neither rod nor child was spared. The little pitchers were taken firmly by the ears while the facts were poured in. Children were to be heard only in answer to questions. They were not to whisper in the classroom, nor speak in the corridor, nor shout in the school yard. They may have read Nick Carter behind the barn, but the social conspiracy was to make them into Little Rollos and Little Lord Fauntleroys. A dozen school years of living under such assumptions brought them to college relatively acquiescent and uninquiring, except of each other and of books.

The sons have fared quite differently. About the time their fathers came out from college the schoolteacher arrived at last at a realization of what the poet had been saying for centuries: that the child was in fact an irrepressible; that for his own soul's salvation he must be heard; that instead of being an empty little pitcher he was a full little teakettle with steam up. So the kindergartner taught the grade-school teacher, and the grade-school teacher taught the parent, and the word was passed along till Montessori and Stanley Hall gained a hearing where Pestalozzi and Horace Mann had been denied one; and in the course of ten years the whole educational world was busy providing devices for tipping the lid of the teakettle. They were agog with educational catchwords: the gospel of self-expression, adolescence, mental therapeutics, and, finally, glands; while they salvaged the gang by means of the Boy Scouts and the Campfire Girls, and organized play till they reached its apotheosis in the summer camp at forty a week plus traveling expenses plus a khaki suit plus a tin cup, a teaspoon, and two blankets.

It is no wonder that in such circumstances the son feels somewhat freer than his father did. But there is a further reason. For the elder generation has not only stimulated a spirit of challenge; it has provided youth with an unparalleled array of conditions that call for challenge. One has only to think of the difference between the dozy complacency of the world in which the men of the nineties grew up and the confusion into which their sons have been plunged. The boys leaving college in 1927 were five years short of high school in 1914. Since then they have seen as a background for all their living four years of World War and nine years of aftermath. If in the face of general conditions they should feel that this is the best of all possible times in the best of all possible worlds, it is patent that they would better not waste their days trying to cope with either facts or ideas. But if they do not feel that this is the best of all possible times in the best of all possible worlds, the spirit of expression that education has been developing in them must lead them to acknowledge that the world is in an unhappy plight, and must lead them to place the responsibility on the elder generations and in some degree on the generation just ahead of them.

Normal youth has always been doomed to pass through a zone of disillusionment and misanthropy. "Goodbye, proud world! I'm going home," or "The world is too much with us, getting and spending," or "Wherever I go, men pursue me and paw me with their dirty institutions, and try to constrain me into their desperate odd-fellow society." It is a part of life. Yet many adults fail to understand it in its aggravated form today, and fail to realize that if they were any good as college boys they went through the same experience in some milder degree themselves. Instead they scoff at the boy who turns his back on life in disgust pouring contempt on it all as "a cascade of accidents, exasperated by policemen," and they sneer at the young Hamlet who comes back to a sense of social responsibility with the sad conclusion that the time is out of joint, and who curses the spite that ever he was born to set it right.

It follows naturally that, among other objects of criticism, youth looks askance at education. "Human experience is interesting," they say, "though not particularly edifying, but what does it lead to? What are the implications to be drawn from it? What right have our elders to impose their interpretations on us? Or as far as that goes, to impose their theory of education or their idea of a college?" And now as they talk with ill-concealed or unconcealed hostility, middle-age finds it hard to regard them with charity. It is easier to take refuge in indignation. "Charity," says middle-age, "they need it! They are everything that charity is not. 'Charity suffereth long and is kind. Charity is not puffed up; doth not behave itself unseemly, is not easily provoked. Charity beareth all things, endureth all things, hopeth all things, believeth all things.' But modern youth says, "'I'll be damned' and 'Tell it to the marines.' " It goes without saying that such an exchange of amenities does not go far toward the establishment of cordial relations. Peace was never made that way between the pot and the kettle.

I submit, as one who pleads guilty to middle-age, that this state of affairs offers a very stimulating challenge. Grant that the picture is exaggerated and that there are thousands of students who are more amenable. Still, broadly speaking, these conditions are true of the stronger element in college, and the only intelligent course is to meet them more than halfway. Here are two sage comments that oddly enough were made years apart by a distinguished father and a twentieth-century son. Said the father one time when I had been speaking intolerantly of some difficult people with and through whom I was trying to work, "You'll never accomplish much with other people until you learn to deal with human beings as forces of nature." And the son, then a first drawing Phi Beta Kappa in an old-line eastern university, "Down here they tell you

they want you to use your own mind as long as you
don't. Then they say, 'You'll know better when
you're as old as we are!'" Put these two remarks together and you will find a justification for the attitude toward his students of a great contemporary
teacher who said years ago, "I never face a new class
without remembering that there may be at least two
minds in it that are potentially better than my
own."

An attempt to be sympathetic with college insurgents does not mean regarding them as demigods.
If there were anything to be gained from drawing
an indictment against them, there are plenty of dam-
aging things to be said. Many of them want to discuss fundamental principles without mastering the
fundamental body of fact on which discussion
should rest. They want to plunge into higher
mathematics without stopping for the multiplica-
tion table. Many of them read extensively in current literature, though they are very far from well-
read. There is more or less wrong-headedness and
some positive perversity among them. Some of them
are proud of their abandonment of faith. They are
mechanists and behaviorists and utilitarians and
futilitarians. Yet all things considered they are not
much less reasonable than middle-age. They are
skeptical about general conditions because the world
is reasonably far away from the millennium as yet.
They are critical of the theory and the processes of
education for the same good reason that every en-

lightened educator is—because these, too, are subject to improvement. It is only while they are being treated as creatures of a low order of intelligence that they are rebellious—only as long as the elders say or imply that they will surely see things as age sees them when they are as old as we are.

Here, for example, and they could be multiplied indefinitely, is a bit out of a letter from a young irreconcilable, the kind who at one stage in his career assumes that all professors are simpletons and most of them natural foes. Of course he is no longer irreconcilable or he wouldn't be writing, yet still in character he starts off with a cheery blast just as a reminder of what a bold, bad boy he is. Halfway down, however, he pauses: "On reading this over I have to smile. To rail at the uninterest and the unintelligence of others, presumes a vast degree of prodigity in oneself, doesn't it?" He goes on, "We were all equally dumb when we arrived at college, and all equally disdainful of books and learning." And then, "Queer how some change and some don't. Boy up the hall aways—came to college determined to go to ——— and become a mechanical engineer. Now a Senior and still holds to that—also to all pre-college belief in the essential goodness of the world and the hallowed sanctity of the Republican party. No doubts. Boy right across the hall—playing a rotten saxophone—came to college as the purest, fairest flower we ever had. Cringed when one swore —went to church because he liked it—and every night knelt down beside his bed and said his prayers. Lately he has fallen heir to a little of Mark Twain's pessimism—taking college rough-house of beliefs too seriously." The "college rough-house of beliefs" is an inspired phrase, for the rough-house is the spontaneous letting off of surplus energy when the hair gets mussed and the clothes get rumpled and when sometimes tempers get roused and what started as play comes very near to being a fight. But the normal youngster learns first to take rough-housing in the right spirit, not too seriously, and later outgrows it altogether after gaining much in the experience.

The history of Mathers from beginning to end has been a history of orthodoxy and dissent. That is why there seems to be so little need to distrust the saving power of tradition or to fear the insurgence of youth. Dough is sadly unwieldy stuff without its yeast; and Mathers, as a lively and typical American college, needs both and has always had both.

CHAPTER VI

The Public and the Reading Public

I N 1911 Theodore Dreiser's *Jennie Ger-hardt* was published and received with acclaim; before the applause subsided it was discovered that eleven years agone his *Sister Carrie* had been published and suppressed—auto-suppressed—without exciting attention by either event. When reprinted it was applauded as vigorously as the companion book. In 1915 Edwin Arlington Robinson's *Captain Craig, a Book of Poems* appeared and was highly commended. On the back of the title-page the fact is recorded that the volume was copyrighted in 1902; and the fact is worthy of record that it was ignored on publication by all except a few faithful friends and except Theodore Roosevelt, who forthwith became a faithful friend. In 1913 and 1914 Robert Frost's *A Boy's Will* and *North of Boston* were published in London and shortly thereafter in New York. *North of Boston* soon went into a second edition; but Robert Frost had been writing in the same vein for twenty years before he won a hearing in the United States. In 1915 Edgar Lee Masters' *Spoon*

River Anthology was a sensation of the year. Next year came *Songs and Satires*, from which the critics selected for special commendation certain poems which showed that Mr. Masters could write in the established form as well as in free verse; but the poems that they commended had been in a volume of 1898 which had received no attention from the critics to whom it was sent for review. One could go considerably further reciting facts of this sort. They all point in one direction: toward the conclusion that, whatever else had happened in the United States in the first fifteen years of the century, surely something had happened to the public to awaken it to home-bred, independent writers whom it had previously been content to ignore.

One thing to do with a conclusion of this sort is to adopt it into the miscellaneous family of one's ideas, bid it mind its *p*'s and *q*'s, and call it out from time to time to speak its little piece before friends and visitors. But a child that is worth adopting is sooner or later bound to become inquisitive about its parentage, and a modern child will not be put off with genial evasions. This youngster is a gamin of the lecture hall, the library, the news-stand and the smoking-room. It raises questions insistently. Since 1900 something seems to have happened to the American imagination so that the public is reading the sort of literature that it used to neglect. What has happened—what could happen to the American imagination? What is the public? What is reading?

The Public and the Reading Public

The conventional way of putting off the inquisitive small boy is to tell him to ask his father. It can't be done this time, for the finding of father is the point of all the questions. There is no decent way out of looking into the facts, of asking questions for oneself. However, to put such questions to oneself—honestly, and not for purposes of justifying a ready-made conclusion—stirs up a hornet's nest of confusing answers. Out of the hubbub it appears first of all that the imagination of the country has been affected in two ways: it has been dulled if not deadened, and it has been very much stimulated. Both these effects could conceivably be wrought on the same subject alternately or in conflict; but a little thought makes it clear sooner or later that the deadening effects have been exerted mainly on the public as a whole, and that the stimulating effects have been felt by what may be called the "reading public."

It is a parlous matter to attempt definitions of such terms as "reading" and the "reading public"; yet for purposes of discussion it must be said that by "reading" is meant the capacity and the readiness to read print which is provocative of thought, and that by the "reading public" is meant the minority who do actually read such print. This beats the devil around the bush by the resort to so vague a phrase as "provocative of thought," and again there is no escape from being somewhat arbitrary.

A survey of the best-sellers since 1900 eliminates

from the picture the public who buy only these books. Of about a hundred and fifty works listed in the first twenty years of the century it would a liberal interpretation that regarded a quarter of them as even seriously intended. The appearance in the favored list of a few books to which one could give a second thought, or even discuss after dinner when glib talkers discuss the books that "everybody" except themselves has read, proves that there has never been an absolute popular embargo on books with style and substance. It is evident, though, that the thousands will read books only if they are in some way relevant to matters of immediate interest. With the Spanish War fresh in mind buyers did well by novels of early American life. An assault on the wheat speculators made a success of *The Pit;* on the meat-packers, of *The Jungle;* on the ways of the specious religionist, of *The Inside of the Cup*. Out of the World War emerged *Mr. Britling*, and out of the return to normalcy *Main Street* and *Babbitt*. But these stories strive in vain to hold their own against *Molly Make-Believe* and *Pollyanna*, *The Harvester* and *Barbara Worth*, *The Black Bag*, *The Blue Flower*, *The Red Planet*, and *The White Mice*. Unfortunately for purposes of comparison the best-seller lists have separated non-fiction from fiction, with no indication as to whether essay, poetry, and drama ever vied in actual circulation with the charmed first six. Unfortunately, too, the Pulitzer prize in fiction has been offered not for the best American novel of the year, but for novels of wholesome American atmosphere and noble manhood, so that comparison between jury decisions and buyers' markets is lost. But probably little would be gained from the additional data.

There is no use pretending that either the theory of equality or the experience of a century and a half of democracy has developed any high level of aesthetics in America. Yet somewhere, partly overlapping this best-seller class, is another, best-reader class, large enough to make a market that will commercially justify publication of good books. There may be inglorious Miltons in the country today, but if they are mute they are not often mute for lack of a publisher. Most American writers of reputation are far from unrewarded even when their writing was not chiefly motivated by the desire for reward. And this best-reader class in its present dimensions is relatively new in the United States. They are reading history, and the newer works in science, and encouraging new editions of neglected authors, and supporting poets and dramatists and story-tellers and even critics. There may be a quarter of a million of them altogether, maybe not but a hundred thousand, maybe only half that. Whatever the total is there was no such number buying books of substance a quarter of a century ago, And the people who have been reading Keynes and Strachey and Dean Inge and Henry Adams and Slosson and Wiggam and Bertrand Russell and John Dewey are in the main the same people who are showing authors and publishers a measurable zest for pure literature, for books that are well written and that are provocative of thought because of an intelligent and honest approach to life.

The leveling and standardizing process affecting the nation as a whole has had its meed of attention; but the stimulation of independent thought has not been mentioned, largely perhaps because the only people interested in this are the people who have felt it and do not need to be told that they are awake. Yet both the unintellectual masses and the intellectual classes have changed within the last twenty-five years; and both sets of changes are worth observing.

II

The influences toward standardization have been so often mentioned of late and are so obvious that one of the most emphatic ways of presenting them is to picture a United States that knew none of them. Here are a few sentences from an essay on *What Is an American?* composed about a hundred and fifty years ago: "The American is a new man, who acts upon new principles; he must therefore entertain new ideas and form new opinions. . . . . As citizens it is easy to imagine that they will carefully read the newspapers, enter into any political disquisition, freely blame or censure governors and others. . . . . As Christians, religion curbs not in their opinions; the general indulgence leaves everyone to think for themselves in spiritual matters; the laws inspect our actions, our thoughts are left to God. . . . . Exclusive of these general characteristics, each province has its own, founded on the government, climate, mode of husbandry, customs and peculiarity of circumstances. . . . . Whoever traverses the continent must observe these strong differences, which will grow more evident in time." If this, which was written a long time ago, seems like anything but a characterization of America today, a second observation written over a hundred years later, seems almost as romantically far afield: "Public opinion grows more temperate, more mellow, assuredly more tolerant. Its very strength disposes it to bear with opposition or remonstrance. It respects itself too much to wish to silence any voice." Viscount Brice, writing just before the turn of the twentieth century, is nearly as wide of the mark today as St. Jean de Crèvecœur, writing just before the outbreak of the Revolutionary War.

There is nothing new, and nothing particularly informative, in re-enumerating the forces that have turned to naught these expositions of America. Yet they must be mentioned again in any attempt to answer the questions that have been raised. Many as they are, they fall into groups that make them seem, perhaps, a bit less momentous than in an undistinguished list. The simplest are the material changes that have brought the rural fireside and the city radiator nearer to the town pump and the soldiers' monument: the rural free postal delivery, and the telephone which came with the century, the cheap motor car, and the good road development which followed hard after; and, with the cheap magazine delivered at the fireside and the village square brought within easy distance, all the machinery of national advertising and of mail-order and chain-store distribution. It is needless to dwell on the results. The advertising pages of any popular magazine and the shop windows on any village square will tell the story.

People who eat and drink the same supplies and wear and use the same clothes and utensils will turn to the same diversions. On the village square is the movie-house. They say at Hollywood that no big production is a success until it has reached nine million people. Up to the present one must go to Main Street to see the film; but the rest of the machinery has reached the fireside itself. What is home without a talking machine, or life without a radio? But with the radio and the talking machine home is just what the drug store is—where one hears the song hit of the week as he messes with the latest ice-cream combination—or the barber-shop, or the dance hall, or the church sociable, or anybody else's home, where "listening in" is offered as an easy substitute for conversation or furnishes an obligato to the exchange of gossip. And at home, by the family lamp, the local newspaper furnishes in the patent insides the same syndicated verse, the same bromidic homilies, and the same comic strips from one end of the country to the other. The daily pabulum supplied Americans of modest income who live in modest houses or apartments and own modest cars and cherish modest ambitions is furnished by Mack Sennett and Harold Lloyd, Edgar Guest and Walt Mason, Sidney Smith and Bud Fisher, Frank Crane and Parkes Cadman, Irving Berlin and Paul Whiteman, and it is furnished all these modest Americans on the same days in the same forms.

Uniformity of thinking, or what passes for thinking, is a natural consequence of all this. The courthouse square still echoes to the refrains that became familiar in 1917 and 1918, sprung from the impulse then to enlist all efforts toward a common end and to discourage any asking of questions or airing of opinions. To question as to the righteousness of the war was to be a traitor; to inquire openly as to its objectives was to be burned in effigy; to withhold from investment in war-loan securities was to invite ostracism; and the prolonged imprisonment of political offenders and conscientious objectors has found no parallel in Europe. This, though vicious, was normal at the time; but the "return to normalcy" has brought no general return to toleration of divers opinions, for America is now in the actually normal post-bellum period of hysterically reactionary conservatism. Zealous patriotism is trying to convert the Declaration of Independence and the Bill of Rights into seditious utterances, and organizations have multiplied in behalf of hundred per cent Americanism, all ostensibly founded for the promotion of positive ends, but all repressive in intention and many lawless in procedure. With one extraordinary exception, dominant public opinion has been arrayed behind a conservative government, with the reigning purpose of keeping cool with Coolidge and making it hot for the opposition. No one must rock the boat, no one must advocate swapping horses while crossing a shoreless stream, no one must embarrass the administration.

So public opinion, the public opinion of the village square, exhilarated by the exercise of its own power, has been exploited for the extension of every kind of legislative control. The activities of the Fundamentalists have been quite in tune with the activities of the Ku Klux Klan, and not out of harmony with the activities of the dwindling American Legion, the Minute Men of Concord, and other organizations and movements of the sort. They have exerted an immense influence—though their influence has elicited a strong reaction which belongs to the other side of the story. With them the list of standardizing forces may end. There is so little question as to their cumulative power that they do not need to be expounded; listing is enough. They have been exerted on a public which includes in its number the makers of best-sellers in the book world, commonplace buyers for the most part of commonplace books.

But they have totally failed to repress a smaller body of writers and readers who are the subject of this meditation.

III

Macaulay never spoke more sanely than when he said that logicians may reason about abstractions, but that the great mass of men must have images. He might have gone further to say that even when the images appear in the shape of leaders the abstractions behind them can be brought home to the great mass only when they are related to affairs of immediate moment and demonstrable interest. Yet there is a body of people between the technical logicians and the crowd to whom abstractions are not uninteresting: the lusty conservative and the excited liberal who do not rely wholly on their emotions, and the element among the middle-of-the-roaders who are where they are through caution rather than through inertia. The most aggressive of contemporary critics are so busy shooting at the barn-door target of popular ignorance and stupidity that they have no time to notice the people who are giving them an audience, an audience that they could not have secured a decade or two ago.

National self-consciousness began to awake from a long sleep in the United States in the midst of the eighteen nineties. Howells' *Traveler from Altruria* brought an indictment against the behavior of American democracy. Bryce's *American Commonwealth* interpreted its essential theories. The Vene-

zuela episode reminded the average citizen that the
magnificent isolation fallacy could not be cherished
indefinitely. Richard Olney, Cleveland's secretary
of state, specifically repudiated it. Soon came the
Spanish War, a burst of jingoism, a burst of self-
complacency, and a popular enthusiasm for America's picturesque past that bought a million-and-a-
third copies of four historical novels published between 1899 and 1901. And then an image appeared
in the form of Theodore Roosevelt with a big stick
in one hand and a lash for the muckrakers in the
other. Magazines flourished on agitation. Ida Tar-
bell, Ray Stannard Baker, and Lincoln Steffens
shook people up with their articles in the *American*.
Thomas W. Lawson jumped the circulation of *Everybody's* so fast as nearly to ruin it with the prosperity begotten of "Frenzied Finance." *Collier's* un-
dermined the security of the Taft administration
with its assaults on the Secretary of the Interior.
For a moment there was a third party. It was only
a dramatic threat, but it was dramatic enough to
catch the attention of the country, and though the
populace quickly forgot, all these utterances and
events recruited a body of readers who were aware
that for better or for worse life was more interesting than they had suspected, and that life in America was by no means devoid of color.

This American self-consciousness, further stimulated by Englishmen like Wells and Bennett and
Dickinson who were for dragooning America into

self-respect, drew a fresh body of readers to American biography. The lives of Andrew D. White and John Hay gave a good many contemporaries their first inkling of foreign relations and of how the devious diplomatic game is played, and awakened an interest that was to continue all the way to the letters of Lane and Page. The stories of Carl Schurz, Booker Washington, and Jacob Riis satisfied the romantic, New World zest for the up-from-poverty theme, as Carnegie did more crassly, and Bok more complacently and Pupin most significantly. The accumulations of vast fortunes, chronicled from various points of view, held the multi-millionaires up to the light both as buccaneers and as sources of retributive benefactions. Sage and Rockefeller furnished chapters in the history of the trust-busters even while they were setting the pace in welfare endowments for which history offers no parallel; and the thoughtful were edified both by their tactics and their scruples. Here and there people read the remarkable but neglected autobiography of William J. Stillman, and everywhere they read *The Education of Henry Adams*, which presented none of the qualities or achievements that are usually cited as American, was skeptical of the whole thesis of democracy, with no tinge of optimism, efficiency, self-assurance, or religious orthodoxy, and which sold like a successful novel and was discussed on every side and understood by a few of the least loquacious.

The Spanish War had been responsible for one

glorious Fourth, but after a year pink pop and fire-
crackers had come to their own again with the people—of, by, and for whom a government had been
founded; unless to the more privileged it meant, in
the eloquent words of a haberdasher's advertise-
ment, "the sweet crack of a cleanly hit ball . . . .
the salty tang of a white-plumed wave . . . . the
soothing hum of a well-tuned motor." Four months
of excitement and two naval engagements had not
been enough to put any meaning into such a phrase
as "international relations." For almost everybody
the word "imperialism" was no more than a vague
sound. Even the limited reading public were content with personal chronicles as vehicles of American history, until with the Mexican-border troubles
the national imagination was jogged again. The
picturesque energies of Roosevelt had sought in vain
for an adequate outlet. He had brandished a big
stick in mid-air but had had to be content with
wielding a busy broom; and housecleaning, even in
its most strenuous moments, is no more than a negative, indoor disturbance. The big chance was denied to the Roosevelt of the third party and offered
to the Wilson of the opposition, and he responded
not with either club or broom, but with pen—
a sequence of slogans on "Watchful Waiting,"
"Being Too Proud to Fight," "Making a World
Safe for Democracy," and "Waging a War to End
War."

The fact of the war and the appeals of the latter

slogans was followed by a succession of moods and convictions: The world was to be jumped three or four centuries toward the millennium in three or four months. It ought to be, even if it would not. It should have been, even if it had not. And finally came the confirmed pessimism or the incorrigible optimism of the tough- or tender-minded post-bellum philosophers. Whatever their conclusions, Americans who where capable of any thought were brought nearer to reality than Americans had been for two generations, and the eclectic reading public had been inured to the reading of pages that had some substance and some vitality in them.

The speculation stimulated on social theses during the war opened the way to speculation in other fields. `Mass bereavement reawakened the interest in spiritualism which had been better than dormant just before. Mass neurosis provoked a fresh enthusiasm for every form of applied and misapplied psychology. Where the psychologists stopped, the physiologists began. Where the physiologists flagged, the biologists continued. And when the biologists had done, the physicists, with their revolutionizing theory of the constitution of matter, converted the human body into a system of gyrating electrons as complex and as restless as the stellar universe. This explorative approach to the world of matter and the mind of man was not confined to the laboratory or the scientific monograph. The indefatigable Wells and his *Outline of History* achieved an unprecedented army of readers and passed regiments of them on to Van Loon and Thompson, Freud and Jung, Slosson and Wiggam, Robinson, Russell and Durant.

A recital of this sort, if one knew nothing of the present, might seem to be leading up to the millennial climax of intellectual activity—to the America of new principles and new opinions announced by Crèvecœur, or to the mellowed, temperate, tolerant public opinion described by Bryce. As a matter of fact, of course, nothing of the kind has eventuated. America, measured by the millions, is no more alert than it was in 1900. It does not read. It does not think. From the newspaper it gets dabs of sifted and colored fact; from the popular magazines and the moving pictures, dabs of moralized or demoralized emotion. And yet within the country, within the literate, adult portion of it, and within that portion of the reading public which patronizes the best-sellers, there is an increasing little minority of people who are wondering about themselves and the circumstances in which they are living, and who care to read such books as may throw light on the mystery.

A single factor remains, already mentioned as the last factor in the standardizing of American thought. For the return to normalcy movement has cut two ways. To a lamentable degree it has herded the majority on to a rationalized justification of things-as-they-are, in the state, in the market, in the

church, the school, and the family. But the attempt
of solicitous conservatism not only to have its own
way but withal to silence free inquiry and free criticism has resulted in a beneficent definition of issues
and a reassuring alignment of forces. The stupid
identification of intelligent liberalism with redness,
with bolshevism, and with that idiotic compound
"anarchy'n-socialism" has forced the liberal to
stand for the right to think and speak, and to de-
fend the freedom of the man who chooses to read
the Declaration of Independence and the New Testament as well as to revere them, or the woman
who wants to know about her place in the social
order and her obligations to it, or the wage-earner
who asks for a definition of an infant industry,
or the boys and girls who query as to the purpose
and procedure of the education in which they are
involved.

There have always been such inquirers about, and
they will never amount to more than a wisp of a
minority; but of late they have been impelled to
mobilize in America, and their mobilization has as-
sembled a discriminating group of readers. For their
concern with life leads the more imaginative of them
straight to art, whose function it is to cope with life
either by coming to grips with it or affording an
escape from it. The result is that men and women in
the United States today can write without concession to popularity, and if they write well and truly
they can win a response that will not only encourage

them to go on, but will more than keep them out of the poorhouse. Life flows along and most men and women drift along with it as they have always done and always will do; but these latter years have set a few of them to thinking, more than usual, and they are the best-readers.

CHAPTER VII
Joseph Hergesheimer

As each flower upon the fresh hill-side
And every colored petal of each flower,
Is sketched and dyed each with a new design,
Its spot of purple and its streak of brown
So each man's life shall have its proper lights,
And a few joys, a few peculiar charms.

THIS is what Ralph Waldo Emerson wrote of Joseph Hergesheimer, though neither probably ever made the application; Waldo certainly not, for Joseph was two years old when the poet died. Nor has Joseph probably recognized what a perfect gloss he wrote on these lines in his opening pages of *San Cristobal de la Habana*.

He has arrived one day in Havana. He goes to his hotel, dresses for dinner, and partakes of his meal; and he writes at length of the experience. For the average traveler, for even the average traveler with more than average keenness of observation and gift of phrase, the first hours in Havana would be pervaded with a consciousness of the difference between this place and other places, with the look of the harbor, the docks, the streets, the hotel lobby, the people and their costumes and manners. But "we are what we are made," and this particular traveler postpones the thought of these broader aspects of the picture. For the moment he has to adjust himself to new and near surroundings, and he has to prepare himself for a ritual. So at the outset his eyes are chiefly for his room. He likes its high coolness and the splashes of light that slant across the wall through a vari-colored lunette. His spirit can repose here; so he lays out his clothes, bathes his body, dresses, with especial attention to the texture and tone of his scarf, experimenting gravely until he is satisfied. He descends to the dining-room, achieves the proper table for enjoyment of the proper food and drink, and proceeds to the ritual of the meal itself. This is not a vast Dickensian repast but a sequence of delectations for an unjaded palate. And after it, in the soft twilight, with the lighting of the proper cigar, he sends up fragrant incense to the minor but important god of gustation.

Restating the facts does not re-create the tone. What Mr. Hergesheimer accomplishes with such detail is to raise in the minds of appreciative readers a sense of perfect appropriateness. They may realize that they could never partake of a meal with this fulness of relish, just as they may realize that they never could feel the original zest of a poet. But they at least vaguely associate the joys of the palate with the joys of the spirit. As a result of their reading

they may conclude to seize the day or they resolve
to mortify the flesh (Joseph would be indifferent, for
he has no desire to influence them); and they may
recall (with whatever innuendo they qualify the re-
collection) that Waldo said of the hypocritic days:
"To each they offer gifts after his will."

II

To the author of *Linda Condon* life has become in
all its hours a refinement of sensuous experiences.
Food is only incidentally sustenance. The clothes
that supply warmth and protection should be pleasant to see and touch. And a house is less than nothing if it is conceived of only as a shelter. It is an expression of the complete man, the resort in which
his soul expands, an asylum of the spirit. For this
American, used to the amplitudes and the amenities
from childhood, a house must be incarnate age and
rock-bound stability. In the perpetuation of the
past it must give grounds for criticism of the present.
It must be so stable that it receives only on suffer-
ance the resident of the moment. And it must be exacting in its demands on him, reaching out through
him and securing from their hiding places in the
past the chairs and tables and chests and rugs and
pewter and glass that inevitably belong to it. It
must be the work of art that life itself should be,
surrounded by turf and tree and plant and shrub that
perennially renew the past and beautify the passing
moment. It must form the motivation for the liter-

ary art of the writer in it, so that he writes to support it, gathers data in its interest, brings his rewards to its hearthstone as to an exacting mistress, and finds that for his own reward he has "a house to live in that upholds him with an inviolable whispered calm."

The calm that comes to him is born of the fact that the house prolongs the quiet of an early Quaker pastoral in the midst of a tumultuous present, and that it promotes the spirit of the patriot, as that spirit roots itself in the love of the land and the fireside, depresses him with a sense of the social disintegration now in process, and reawakens in him the faith of the federalist, who is nearest to the traditions that prevailed when the house was builded, and who is most skeptical about the democratic experiment that would in time substitute bungalows and flats for homesteads that stand foursquare against the winds of innovation.

So he installs himself in such a homestead (and he tells all about it in the pages entitled "From an Old House"—though oddly enough they were not written from it but from a rented room in the town), and once installed here, he weighs past and present in the balance. He is a Presbyterian child of a rich, aristocratic past, the kind of past to which Linda Condon, born of the Lowries, returned when she became Linda Hallet. What he cherishes from this past is not the religious belief but the capacity for enjoyment, and an admiration for the independence of mind and action that belongs to the well-in-trenched aristocrat. He misses just these traits in the present. He knows very well that his father and grandfather would look askance at his writings. His grandfather would detest *Cytherea*, regard *Linda* as a mad performance, and pass *The Lay Anthony* without a word. He would approve the back-grounds of *The Three Black Pennys*, *Java Head*, and *Balisand;* but *Mountain Blood* he would fully under-stand because it is so completely Presbyterian.

The judgment of the past—the Dower House of his imagination—would accord him no great hon-ors. He has no great respect for the judgment of the present; but fortunately it is a lavish one, for it sup-plies him the wherewithal for quietude and spa-ciousness of surroundings, escape from intolerable people and conditions, and the privacy and freedom in which he can devote himself to putting into words the thoughts that intrigue him. This re-sponse of the public is the more fortunate because he has not agreed with them in their formula for the desirable story, and he has not intentionally com-pounded with them. He does not see many heroes about him, and he tries to write of the kind of peo-ple he has seen. Not being heroes the men do not achieve prodigies of valor or any victories greater than that of maintaining their own integrities; so that Mr. Hergesheimer has had to overcome the re-pute of being a dealer in unhappy endings. And the women that he writes of do not please the women, because, as an old Tory, he prefers his women characters to be rather more charming than efficient, which seems belittling to the modern feminist. But he has gone on his way, a little amused and a little surprised that he has cleft the rock of prejudice with so slight a weapon as his pen and that an increasing rivulet of gold is flowing therefrom.

In a passage of self-analysis Mr. Hergesheimer makes himself imperatively quotable on the subject of his characters: "I didn't particularly, the truth was, admire my own character; I should not—except for the ability of work—have chosen it. I liked calmness and I wasn't calm; I liked fidelity, and except to my writing, I wasn't conspicuous for it; I liked hardness of body, a condition I hadn't the perseverance to keep; I liked, for myself, in vain, a distinguished resolution in bearing and mind." So, lacking these characteristics himself, he says, they seemed uncommonly desirable to him, and he made them live on paper. But he omits from this passage another trait which does belong to himself—a highly developed formality coupled with an inherent independence of mind and conduct. It is the heritage of the non-conformist aristocrat. It belongs to all the black Pennys, but no less to Isabel Penny who is the product of supercultivation yet resiliently strong as a Damascus blade. It belongs to Linda Hallet, who, like Isabel, could with unraised pulse defy her husband in behalf of palpitant youth. It is a part of Richard Bale, who on the morning of a duel to the death can tell his wife only by indirection of his sentiment, too deep for words, which possesses him for his home and his homestead. It is a part, and the larger part, of Tao Yuen, who comes from a civilization measured by millenniums and whose implicit but unmistakable vitality is never betrayed into outward expression. These characters are all the natural creations of an author who could say for himself, "A complete formality, it seemed to me, provided a mask behind which the individual could rest, retire, unwearied by the endless fatigue of personal contacts."

He surrounded himself with complete formality in architecture and furniture, and dominated by that portion of himself which is his home, he resolved after early wanderings of the imagination never again in his writing to depart from the traditions of America, to stray from the mood of Dower House. It is a mood not dissimilar to that of *The House of the Seven Gables*, a mood which can be re-created from the past of all the seaboard towns from Salem to New Orleans. Yet he did not do this with the resolution of the historical novelist. He had rather chosen—or acknowledged—the idiom in which he must write, and was concerned with the facts only as they were expressive of the mood. Fancy could create a background which never was on land or sea, like the exotic backgrounds of Poe, but imagination can act as Hawthorne's did, and connect "a bygone time with the very present that is flitting away from us," prolonging a legend, to continue with Hawthorne's words, "from an epoch now gray in the distance, down into our own broad sunlight, and bringing along with it some of its legendary mist." As the mood is timeless and as the idiom is only that of thought and action, Mr. Hergesheimer, like Hawthorne, speaks in the language of his own day, in the perennial idiom of good English, abjuring the archaisms of the past. And the perennial idioms of life are expressed, partly in fine capacities to enjoy the best of life's sights and sounds, and partly in finer capacities for strength and constancy and courage.

Like Hawthorne again, he seldom forgets that "the very present is flitting away from us." It is an inevitable feeling for characters whose eyes are focused on the past. There is a minor key prevailing through his pages, the key sounded on the entrance of Jasper Penny, "conscious of the invidious beginning weariness of accumulating years," and on the entrance of Richard Bale, just past thirty but weary of the strife of years, aware that life has but the frail duration of a flower, and that the finest quality of a flower is its fragrance. To Jasper and Richard a renewal of youth is offered and mockingly withheld. The hand of the past is on them both as the present slips away.

Richard Bale, if he could have lived as far north as West Chester, would have felt at home in the Dower House. He had fought under Washington, he was a good Federalist, he belonged to the soil, and he loved his country because he loved to feel it under his feet. He fell in love with the betrothed of his host, but delayed in action only long enough to tell of his love and venture his life for it. He could cherish the thought of his heart's desire after her death to the end of his days, and yet be true to his duties as husband, father, lord of a manor. He could live as a type of aristocrat who loved honor and embodied courage, and was all unaware of possessing any fine and lofty sentiments. And withal he could drink and gamble and lose his temper; and he could quarrel superbly. He could fulfil a formula which his literary creator often wanted to fulfil, of portraying courage in the face of disaster, and he could do it in a history that came to no happy ending, but to an ending that was not unheroic.

Around this character there gathers a chronicle that moves unswerving to an inevitable conclusion. Richard Bale, committed to a cause, must follow it at any cost. He may be wrong through ignorance, but convicted of his rightness he is bound to take the chance of sacrificing everything rather than retire in disorder. Worn with the struggle of the Revolutionary War he has passed from a devotion to his native colony through a devotion to Washington to a passionate attachment for a doomed cause—the rule of the aristocracy. A lower order of men are moving into control over the land to which they were indifferent or renegade while the fighting was still on. Weary and heartsick, wishful only for peace on the acres which stand for the traditions of his ancestry, he has to take up the difficulties and the burdens of living. To the new order he is arrogantly and obstinately insufferable. In love and in politics he encounters a rival who seems utterly despicable to him. They go down to death together; but with him the old order passes.

As Richard Bale and his neighbors are anything but simple people, the appropriate style for them is more sumptuous than austere. It is a natural style for a writer who studied painting before he took to the pen, and who has a feeling for surfaces and colors in everything he sees and describes. In every setting for the chronicle there is a sensuous definiteness that lingers in the memory in definite contours and lights and colors. One remembers them as places visited in the flesh, not as persons described. And what might be called the historical details produce not the effect of having been carefully reconstructed so much as the effect of having been definitely recalled. Whether in description or exposition Mr. Hergesheimer has succeeded in his desire "to reproduce in the reader the emotion he would have felt under the same conditions."

If Mr. Hergesheimer can restimulate in the reader the emotions felt by his characters in the quieter scenes and the subtler situations, he is pre-eminently successful in doing this in the more stirring episodes. No one who has read of it can ever quite forget the death of Lavinia Roderick, for he was present on the occasion and felt the fateful horror of it. He has realized it with the same "searing completeness" that Richard experienced at the moment. And no less vivid are the duel of Richard and Gawain Todd, and Gordon Mackimmon's defiance of the mob, and Honora Canderay's lashing of the scandalmonger, and the incomparable fencing episode in *The Bright Shawl*, and a dozen other passages. They are vivid scenes because they were vividly felt by people of keen perceptions and quick responsiveness. They could not have been the same to actors who did not know the speechless dignities and all the finer enjoyments. Mr. Hergesheimer believes, and he shares his belief with many a reader, that the man in the porter's lodge and the man in the garage listen to a more limited language than the man in the Dower House. There are tones they cannot hear, colors that never catch their eyes; and they lose all the emotions these can stimulate in the man who is susceptible to them.

So one came to accept the master of Dower House on his own terms. One thought of him as most at home with the people of his imaginings. There was a clank of the knocker, and he stood in the hall to greet his guests as William opened to them. In came Richard Bale and Lavinia and the sturdy-hearted Lucia, and the three far-separated generations of the Pennys, and Linda Hallet and Arnaud, her husband, and John Woolfolk—all conscious of their forebears but aware of Tao Yuen, Tao Yuen the imperturbable, the only one in whose veins flowed four thousand years of cultural heritage. One could guess at slight surprises and the beginnings of questions, but they were not uttered. At table the talk was of the past, and on the common ground of old tradition there were mellowing responses of word and glance. And finally before the ladies withdrew and the board was cleared there was an instinctive turning toward the lord of the manor. They awaited a toast. He rose and looked about him with the friendly confidence of a youthful patriarch. It was a May evening, and through the open windows the strains of dance music came down from the neighboring clubhouse. The room was aglow with the shaded candlelight which did not quite outshine the twilight gleam of a day that was past. And as his guests turned to him he addressed them with words which from him to them were altogether fitting and proper: "Ladies and gentlemen," he said. . . . .

III

One would like to conclude in such a mood as this, but Mr. Hergesheimer has not been able to resist the march of time even in the home of his imagination, and he has compounded as Richard Bale never would have done, somewhat ignobly, with the present. He has become self-conscious in behalf of Dower House, aware that it is a conspicuous survival from the past. More than that, that it is in fact a restored antique with modern plumbing and electric lights. Below the terrace and the formal garden is the putting green, which means that on a knoll near the first tee, and sheltering the nineteenth hole, is a modern clubhouse. Mr. Hergesheimer writes of an evening when sitting on his terrace alone he hears the music for a party drifting down to him. It is for the casual dancing of the present, millenniums after that of the generations who knew the minuet and immemorially later even than the rhythms of the polka and waltz and schottische. These latter steps are momentarily in the music only to give way to the mad fervors and hysterical moods of negroes at a *danzon*, "a confusion of forms very like the age . . . . the assault of a persuasive discontent."

The phrases which the author applies to the music at the clubhouse may pertinently be applied to what seems to be the trend of his present story-telling, particularly to *Cytherea* and *Tampico*. *Cytherea*, the book, for example, is "a confusion of forms" just as Cytherea, the doll symbol, is "the assault of a persuasive discontent." Lee Random, central figure, a completely modern person with no touch of distinction from the past, has neither calmness, fidelity, hardness of body, nor distinguished reso-lution in his character. Compounded of the op-posites and of a kind of lazily accidental business acumen, he lives in a business world, in a piece of modern domestic architecture, on the edge of a golf course with a wife whom he persists in regarding as a model, although as the story presents her she is unattractive in person and nagging in habit, a potential termagant as events rapidly prove. He is ready for Cytherea, the symbol of alluring womanhood, and for Mrs. Grove, temporary fulfilment of the Cytherean longing. In her he finds a woman who is supreme "on the plane of absolute civilization." She inflames him, not as a potential mother but as a completely seductive being. What now stirred him, says the author, "had nothing to do with breeding." It shortly turns out that it also had nothing to do with good breeding. For the course of Lee and Savina is the course of the clubhouse vulgarians, impossible for the aristocrats of *Java Head* or *Balisand*. It starts with a gross violation of hospitality, slips off into a furtive elopement, and culminates in a fateful orgy of sexual excess. Such things have happened, but they do not happen in these forms to the people of tradition and fine feeling with whom Mr. Hergesheimer formerly consorted on paper.

When in *Cytherea* he abandons the atmosphere of Dower House for the atmosphere of the golf club, he finds, even as he is mounting the hillside, in the rhythm of the dance music, that both roofs shelter at least one thing in common. For "the assault of a persuasive discontent" is the genesis of romantic feeling in all times and all climes. That is what stirs the mountain blood of Gordon Mackimmon, quickens the slow pulse of the pallid aristocrat, Honora

Canderay, and drives Dodge Pleydon, sculptor, and Alexander Hulings, ironmaster, each to his own kind of achievement. In this story Mr. Hergesheimer takes as his setting the hectic and meaningless life of the pleasure-seeker and sets it over against the dream of the unattainable. It is the approach, one cannot help seeing, of Mr. Cabell in the run of his stories—in *The Cream of the Jest*, to cite the most obvious example. Mr. Cabell to reach his end achieves his romance by a flight from Litchfield to Storisende, but eventually finds something in Storisende to reconcile him to Litchfield. The unattainable is actually unattainable; the near approach to any object of desire dissolves the dream and recalls the present, but casts over the present something of the aura of the faraway. The clarity of the stories is comparable to the formula for the square of $x+y$, which is $x^2+2xy+y^2$; the two letters—let them stand as symbols for the near and the remote—overlap but are clearly separable.

It is something of this sort on which Mr. Hergesheimer ventures in *Cytherea*, and which in a virtual epilogue Lee Random struggles in vain to explicate to his astutely drowsy brother. The doll Cytherea has always represented something unknown that he desired. She was a doll, more fascinating than any living woman, but she was a principle. The time came when she was translated into a very individual woman. Lee fell into the error, as he was speculating about the abstract values in life, of putting himself and Savina into the places of x and y. "I . . . . made the mistake of thinking that I, as an individual, had an importance. In my insane belief that a heavenly beauty, a celestial chorus girl, was kept for me, I pictured myself as an object of tender universal consideration." Finally, after the catastrophe, when his wife made a return possible, he had the acumen to see that he could not resume personal relationships with the social order that he had so personally defied. He had rationalized himself out of existence in a concrete world.

But the "assault of a persuasive discontent" is responsible for more than this. In the symbol of Cytherea it made ducks and drakes of Lee Random's career. In the form of twentieth-century dance music it warped Joseph Hergesheimer out of his own orbit. "It hadn't the power to remove me from the terrace, and yet it was vaguely disconcerting." Probably because the assault was not overwhelming but only vaguely disconcerting, the result of it in this novel resembles the music in being "a confusion of forms very like the age." Because of the extraordinary unity of tone and atmosphere that generally prevails in Mr. Hergesheimer's stories, the first impression of this one is of extraordinary disorder. A second tempts one to believe that the disorder was calculated, was inherent in the tale, was artistically inevitable. But a third thought compels one to admit that though the conception is intrinsically sound, the execution is indeterminate and peters out at the end. Fanny, the dull and faithful wife, to play her part in the tale should be impeccable and negatively admirable; but in conduct and in speech she is neither as dull nor as desirable as Lee insists she is. Lee, to be a convincing sport of the gods, should come to a tragic ending. It is in a way tragic that he should resign himself to oblivion and speculate on whether drinking cannot serve him perennially distilled delusions. But no tragedy is complete that is unrecognized by the victim. And no story is tragic in execution that acknowledges by appended pages of exegesis its own failure to convey the point. Cytherea carries an old-fashioned moral, and Mr. Hergesheimer half-heartedly attempts to explain it. It is what the clubhouse did to him with its disconcerting melodies and rhythms. Cytherea only emphasizes the excelling charm of the works that were written in the mood of the old stone pile below the hilltop.

In his first fine fervor for Dower House he once resolved never again to lapse from its mood in his writings, or to depart from the traditions of his country. But, according to his own confession, never conspicuous for fidelity, he ignored this resolution when he wrote *Tampico* and returned to the mood of the clubhouse and the humid sensuousness of Central America. On the surface *Tampico* seems to fit the early Hergesheimer formula, but only on the surface and at first glance. It is in fact a sort of anticlimactic sequel to what the master of Dower House would have done with the same material a dozen years ago. Govett Bradier, when *Tampico* opens, has pursued a career of brilliant and remorseless success as an oil pioneer in Mexico. It is over. He returns to the scene of his triumphs to claim the wife of a friend. He finds himself suspected of business dishonesty toward the man whose love he is despoiling. He is incapable of this particular type of infidelity. In the effort to clear up the charge and the mystery surrounding it, faith unfaithful keeps him falsely true for a while; but this flash of a fine, old integrity is dimmed as he blunders along through malarial attacks, drinking excesses, bawdy-house episodes, and miscellaneous blood-lettings until he loses power, position, the friend, the wife, and slips away furtively from the scene of his defeat with nothing accomplished of what he had come to do.

Tampico is a novel of disintegration which carries with it the uncomfortable suggestion that it is more than a novel—that it is a document in artistic history. All those earlier works of Mr. Hergesheimer, drawn from American history and written in the mood of Dower House, seem vitally different from *Tampico* partly because they are so similar. The central figures are men of achievement, measurably self-controlled but ungovernable by outer control. They behave and misbehave like gentlemen, dominated by a set of convictions about personal honor and sex chivalry and class loyalty that they are willing to die for. These convictions are rather primitive and not very noble, but they are nevertheless ennobling because they stimulate positive faith and positive action. Govett Bradier was a man of this type during his active life as an oil producer before the opening of *Tampico*.

But in this story it is Mr. Hergesheimer rather than Govett Bradier who dominates, and Mr. Hergesheimer is still in the Cytherean mood of a northerner during his early experience in the tropics. It is a common phenomenon in literature. We need go no further than Melville and Hearn for examples. It is featured at first by a delighted acknowledgment of the sensuous opulence of earth, sky, and sea. It is followed by a sensuous relaxation of the usual controls. In the tropic zone the gentleman finds his manners less instinctive than he had thought them in a cooler clime, and his convictions seem of less importance. And when he loses these, as Govett Bradier did, there is nothing left of his well-bred self but an occasional reminiscent gleam of gentility. His drunken boastings and his cheap profanity would disgust Richard Bale. And if Richard Bale would lift an eyebrow and shrug a shoulder at Govett Bradier, so, I think, would Howat Penny at the Hergesheimer who opens a magazine essay with the salute, "I am getting damned tired of art!" Maybe he is; maybe he ought to be, of the pseudo-art which he has in mind; but he expresses himself, in soap-box style, as none of the Pennys would have done.

The Pennys, I take it, and Richard, in loyalty to their old friend would incline very deftly to lure him back to his own manner and his old beliefs. "Come on over to Dower House," they might say. "We picked up an interesting piece in an old shop the other day. We're not quite sure if it's genuine; but you can tell, if anyone can. . . . ."

CHAPTER VIII
Sherwood Anderson

IN HIS *Story Teller's Story*, and in *Tar*, Sherwood Anderson tells very satisfyingly about the things one really wants to know of a story-teller—about how his feeling for life grew into something articulate, and about how the story-telling inclination was born in him and persisted in him now as a dreamer and now as liar, an ornate and disinterested liar, and now as a discontent who did not know that he ought to be doing something particularly different from the thing that did not satisfy him, now as an "ad" writer whose trade value was greater since he was rumored to have sold some fiction but not enough to keep him alive, and finally as a manufacturer who one day discovered that, instead of selling his goods not very fast, he was actually selling his soul. He is quite detached in the telling of it, neither vain nor proud. He gives more space to his father than to anyone else, because he understands the histrionic self-glorification of the man as something that led to story-telling, though to exactly the kind of stories that the son has always abjured.   For he shows that the tales he tells are one with the life he has lived.

This story, like all other good stories, is a record of interesting moments.   And the moments almost always mark a release of the imagination into fields that like as not are unrelated to the circumstances surrounding them.   There is a suspicion of oil in the neighborhood, and a well is to be shot.   The well-shooter becomes a figure of romance and mystery.   His nitro-glycerin brings up nothing but a shower of mud, and he is translated into a villain about whose duplicity the imagination can linger happily.   He is rather more satisfying than a successful well. . . . . The story-teller hates the man working next him in a nail factory and remembers a negro boxer— Harry Walters with the quick shift and the powerful left.   Days of dreaming of the invincible combination lead to the moment of picking a quarrel and the paralyzing defeat that follows. . . . .   He sits before the managers of a concern for which he is to write some advertising.   One of them has a scar almost concealed by his beard.   Into the dim past fades the speaker with all his sales talk, and the "ad" writer dreams the thrilling story that accounts for the scar.

So his imagination gains sway and begins casting around for stories to tell.   They are to be stories in which no man's actions are devoid of beauty, and where the teller himself is consciously a new product in a new land.   This new land turns out to be an in-finitely complicated and puzzling place, as how could it help being when it is peopled by such puzzling and complex units as all men are? It is a country that, first of all, is not England, though the notion that it is, persists incorrigibly. The blood is a mixture of the thin blue of the Puritans and the redder hues of the dreaming nations of the earth. In the mixture he is aware of many elements but never aware of them all at the same time, which is the reason that the resulting compound is so perplexing. Here are the Celts and the Latins and the nations of the Far East pouring their contributions into the veins of America, a love of beauty and song and mirth and of the rightness of things rightly done with capable hands. They are the natural breeders of the artist who is foresworn to his devotion for form and color and for the controlled ecstacy through which he can fulfil himself. They have made the things of lasting beauty and built the great cathedrals at Chartres and Venice and Mont-St.-Michel, and they have worshiped the Virgin. Their peoples have encouraged the artist and enjoyed his work and put up with his vagaries, not taking them too seriously.

And on the other hand, here are the Puritanic English, godly and self-denying and others-denying and fatefully practical, bound always to be doing things for which the artist has no zest; so eagerly efficient that after clearing the forests and building their towns, they set themselves to building up a country to the glory of man, and as earnest about it as the

French were when they builded the Cathedral at
Chartres to the glory of God. This was their plan,
"and the affair only blew up in the process, or got
perverted, because Man, even the brave and free
Man, is somewhat a less worthy object of glorifica-
tion than God." For in the meanwhile the machine
age had killed the best in man.

Unconsciously, in talking of either strain in the
blood of the new America, the story-teller comes
back to God; and it is in this thought that his
puzzlement becomes the greater. The heritage of
the Puritans, he says to himself, was an ungodly
materialism, and the heritage of the Celts and the
Latins was an ungodly paganism. As for himself, he
has no God, the gods having been taken away from
him by the life about him. And yet in a dramatic
moment he says, "I had an odd and to my own seeming, a ridiculous desire to abase myself before something not human, and so stepping into the moonlit
road I knelt in the dust." Never was more devout
an atheist.

Such an atheistical weaver of tales brings his
story to a conclusion exactly where he should—not
to be logical, for I cannot think of his bothering
about that, but to be reasonable, which he doubtless would care to be. For he has become an artist
now and would like to round out the story of his
life with that reasonableness which is the essence
of any work of art. So at the end he is sitting with a
friend before the Cathedral of Chartres where to-

gether they have been worshiping for days. In its presence he feels what the old craftsmen felt who built themselves into the fabric of it. His dream is not theirs but the work of their hands helps him to do what they did—to give shape to his own dream. He cannot be content to sit before the cathedral endlessly dreaming of old days. He must do as they did and live in the moment, in his own country, taking part in its growth. These two worshipers from alien soil must return each to his own place, and he, the story-teller, must reduce his rough material to beauty of form as the stone-carvers had done at Chartres. To the observer who sees him sitting before the cathedral that made him so deeply happy he seems very like those old workmen who took no thought of theology and vented their religion in work. The thoughtful man who calls himself an atheist is often a man who has not found his name for God.

II

The man of such experiences, whatever his religious label may be, is certain to be a mobile character. He will be a man of shifting moods, susceptible to changing conditions and opinions. This country to which he is returning will not present one unchanging aspect to him. In the earlier days when the world of circumstance crowded in too insistently on the story-teller, the thought of the machine seemed almost overwhelming. It was standardizing more than the product, for it was iron-

ing the workmen out all to one size and thickness;
and as they lost their feeling for materials and
their zest in the use of tools, grossness and lewdness
and profanity became the pitiable outlets of their
thwarted selves. It is an abused word these days—
"standardization"—but the story-teller may be
credited with using it to mean the process which
when completed is the outward evidence of inward
dulness. And yet, on second thought, such an interpretation may be more kind than just, for this
story-teller is a poet and a lyric poet at that, using
the same word to mean different things at different
times, not because at any one time the meaning is
blurred in his mind, but because from time to time
his definitions change with his changing opinion of
the world.

Here he is then, thinking about democracy and
the machine and the deadening standardization it is
bringing in its train. It may be that he has just seen
a swarm of men shuffling out of a factory at the end
of a day of meaningless repetitions. What is such
routine going to do to the men and the society they
belong to—those other men in the directors' room
with their meaningless lust for money? "Democracy
shall spread itself out thinner and thinner, it shall
come to nothing but empty mouthings in the end.
. . . . The shrewd little money-getters with the cry
'democracy' on their lips shall rule for a time and
then the real commoners shall come—and that shall
be the worst time of all. Oh, the futile little vanity

of the workers who have forgotten the cunning of hands, who have long let machines take the place of the cunning of hands!'' There was another poet who shared this mood not long ago:

> Shall all the happy shipmates then
> Stand singing brotherly?
> Or shall a haggard ruthless few
>   Warp her over and bring her to
> While the many broken souls of men
> Fester down in the slaver's pen,
>   And nothing to say or do?

That is one mood; but in another the story-teller regains his confidence: "Standardization is a phase. It will pass. The tools and materials of the workmen cannot always remain cheap and foul. If the machine is to survive it will come again under the dominance of the hands of the workman, as it already, no doubt, is doing, in a hundred, perhaps a thousand unknown places. The day of rediscovery of man by man may not be as far off as we fancy." And this, too, that other poet has said:

> For the Brute must bring the good time on; he has no other choice,
> He may struggle, sweat and yell, but he knows exceeding well
> He must work them out salvation ere they send him back to hell.
> .   .   .   .
> Then, perhaps, at the last day,
> They will whistle him away,
> Lay a hand upon his muzzle in the face of God and say,

"Honor, Lord, the thing we tamed!
  Let him not be scourged or blamed,
  Even through his wrath and fierceness was thy fierce wroth
    world reclaimed!"

However, optimism is all very well only so long as it is hardy enough to confront the world of facts. There is an America to be recognized while the struggle is going on between the machine brute and the finer nature of the people. The story-teller can escape into the world of fancy, but even his fancy is built on fact. And perhaps the most salient fact about American life in his opinion is the kind of fancy with which the average American enveils himself. He makes himself a part of a heroic enterprise, a gigantic social experiment in which he assumes that the most unpromising man is a potential hero. The sober fact that this is not true affords him all the more reason for clinging to the fancy, as he has been emboldened to do by a succession of fabulists from Bret Harte to Bill Hart.

So this average American whose zest as a tool-user and maker of things is being blighted by the producing and consuming of cheaply made things is having his imagination standardized. He has created, or more exactly he has adopted, a hero who is interestingly bad but reassuringly good; he is guilty of every sort of offense in the sight of man and God, but he is capable of becoming high and fine at the utterance of the world "mother" or the appearance of a defenseless and immaculate maid.

He is an agreeable fiction but he is a dishonest fiction because he is both so much worse and so much better than the men and women, the novel-readers and showgoers and moving-picture addicts who admire him and sniffle at his nobler manifestations. He is undermining the honesty of a whole people, and laying snares for the story-tellers who might be honest if left to themselves. "As I sat in the movie house it was evident that Bill Hart was being loved by all the men, women and children sitting about and I also want to be loved—to be a little dreaded and feared too, perhaps. 'Ah! there goes Sherwood Anderson! Treat him with respect. He is a bad man when he is aroused. But treat him kindly and he will be as gentle with you as any cooing dove!'"

The Sherwood Anderson who had momentary flashes of desire to be the bold, bad movie hero was making more of an admission than he knew when he confessed to this vain hope. We have all had this sort of furtive wish at the sight of Bill Hart or Douglas Fairbanks or an acrobat or a billiard champion or an All-American halfback. And we have been amused at the feeling as it passed us, and have smiled at it and gone back to selling bonds or making carpet tacks or teaching school. We have made our decision for better or for worse and we have stuck to it. There has been no compounding with fate for us because the thing we yearned for—remotely—was so remote from the thing we were doing.

But for Sherwood Anderson there was a way out. He could do both. What he deliberately chose to do, and what he is doing with almost all his energy, was to become the fine craftsman, working honestly with the rough material of middle western village life and chiseling it into form with the words which are his tools. He wanted to carve out the figures inherent in the stones that lay on every side. He wanted to work in full respect for the fine craftsmanship of the carvers who had wrought before him; not to adopt the mere tricks of a trade but to do the essential thing that they had done. It was life that he was after and not plot. It was the appropriate language that he wanted to use and not literary English. He must never lose his real interest in the people about him; and when he became aware of a story pleading to be told he must lend himself to the simple people who lived it, or might have lived it, and believe in those people until he and they were one. This is the desire of the creative artist and he has striven to fulfil himself in this fashion. But there was still a way out for him when the desire to be bold and bad intrigued him. In the very reality of his people there was an element that the story-tellers just before him had avoided recognizing. The Victorians, on both sides the Atlantic, had been reluctant to acknowledge the persistence of sex feeling. He could maintain his artistic integrity by dwelling on this with ruthless persistence, and he could be a little shocking in the name of art.

Sherwood Anderson

"There goes Sherwood Anderson. He can be a lustful male when he is aroused!"

Mr. Anderson is in fact a sensitive artist and sensitive to most hostile comment. The criticism that any of his characters are not worth putting into fiction hurts him; but the criticism that he is a wicked man with a wicked mind carries no such sting. It may be that he is not fully aware of this himself; just as other men and women are not conscious of the subliminal sex feeling on which he harps; but to the friendly and unshocked observer he does seem to be somewhat Whitmanic in his keeping his hat on indoors or out and sounding his barbaric yawp over the roofs of the world, or raising the roof if he happens to be in the bedroom beneath the eaves. It is too conscious, like the removable front of O'Neill's house under the elms.

I do not mean to be either patting Mr. Anderson on the back, or disposing of this aspect of him with a quip. They are both much too substantial for that. I say merely that the truth lies somewhere between the prevailing implications in many of his pages and the loudest outcries of his most hostile assailants— that the problem does not loom so large as he suggests and that he is not so morbid as they insist. It is a case of overemphasis on both sides. The sex impulse is only one of several dominant desires. Any one of them becomes the more interesting as it pushes its way out of proportion. Perfect balance may serve as subject matter for statuary but literature yearns for ruling passions. For a century and more fiction in English has turned to all the other abnormals but sex abnormals. Now it is paying the penalty for repression which errs as far on one side as current expression does on the other. Among the contemporaries Mr. Anderson is doing his share to restore the balance of the age by indulging in some degree of unbalance in his own work. And he is doing it in a manner that is seldom circumstantial and never sickly. *Winesburg* and *Many Marriages* are quite as healthy as *The Bent Twig* or *The Brimming Cup*. There's "a deal of circumambient hocus-pocus" among the less outspoken writers; and when the balance is restored, as far as Mr. Anderson is concerned,

> . . . . we'll think of what he never said
> Of women—which, if taken all in all
> With what he did say, would buy many horses.

The readers who can see nothing but sex in Anderson's pages—who nudge one with a kind of fearful glee and ask if his latest book is "like all the rest" or "full of his usual preoccupation" or "delves in dark places"—are proof enough that he is writing to some purpose. The very fact that they must always indulge in some shifty periphrasis, cutting circles around the word "sex," shows that the idea behind the word looms ominous in their imaginations, that their preoccupation is possibly no less than his. The best answer to give these peeping Toms of literature, especially if others are within hearing, is to say very audibly that in his latest work sex is just as important and just as unimportant as in all his other books. They never want to pursue the subject when it is brought into the open.

III

Behind and beyond his interest in the relations of men and women, and in the passion which is only a part of love, Anderson is dealing with the whole experience of men and of women, of which love is only a part. In his earlier books, and particularly in *Marching Men*, he seemed to be very much preoccupied with the weighty problems of the industrial order and with a sense of responsibility for setting it right. Society was chaos, the workmen were a wronged body, but a restoration of the rhythm of life was due to set all things in their places in a sentimental millennium. The book seemed almost to be the fruit of varying and unrelated moods—at one time Rousseau and at another Zola, and on the whole Rousseau did him no great service by his intervention. One reads a passage like this and is not stirred: "Chicago is one vast gulf of disorder. Here is the passion for gain, the very spirit of the bourgeoisie gone drunk with desire. The result is something terrible. Chicago is leaderless, purposeless, slovenly, down at the heels. And back of Chicago lie the long cornfields that are not disorderly. There is hope in the corn. Spring comes and the corn is green." Evidently the writer is stirred, but he does not communicate his feeling because he is putting it into worn-out talk. It is soap-box invective against the social order capped with a eulogy on a benignant nature which is fain to teach lessons to a perverse mankind by means of auto-cultured corn crops.

It is a far cry from this sort of writing to the kind that the hero of *Marching Men* was aspiring to: "He wanted his true note as an individual to ring out above the hubbub of voices and then he wanted to use the strength and virility in himself to carry his word far. What he did not want was that his mouth become foul and his brain become numb with the saying and thinking of the thoughts of other men and that he in his turn become a mere toiling food-consuming chattering puppet to the gods." Mr. Anderson did not hit on this true note of his own until he reached the point where he became more interested in what was happening in the minds of his individuals than in what was going on outside their bodies. They were the same people surrounded by the same conditions, but they were no longer mainly significant because they were creatures of circumstance. They might even be such victors over circumstance as Sponge Martin.

Sponge is of all people an unremarkable man to look at or listen to; he is just one more man in a factory, inactive, unprotesting, contented. He lives in a little, old, converted barn on the edge of town with his little, aging, companionable wife. They eat and sleep together, and together they have their occasional sprees that they call "going fishing." Sponge is a competent workman whose hands have become so skilled that he does not need to pay attention to them as his mind runs along in vague memories and his tongue in interminable talk—talk about nothing in particular. To the restless man at the next bench Sponge is a problem. Is he never discontented? Do his job, his wife, his home, satisfy him? Is he satisfied with life?

"Bruce decided that the old man was not necessarily self-satisfied. With him being satisfied or not satisfied did not count . . . . he liked the skill of his own hands. That gave him something to rest on in life. . . . . As to his old woman—there was a thing her man could do better than most men. He rested in that fact and his wife rested in him. The man and the woman had stayed within the limits of their powers, had moved freely within a small but clear circle of life." Sponge and his wife are not merely described and dismissed in *Dark Laughter*, they appear and reappear throughout the story. They are an undercurrent in the book just as they and their kind are an undercurrent in the stream of American life. Many of Anderson's contemporaries are pouring out their scorn on characters who do not know enough to be unhappy. This portrait of the old Martin couple, painted without prejudice, is one of the best in recent literature—a notable picture.

The difference between *Marching Men* and *Dark*

Laughter is parallel to the difference between Anderson the manufacturer and Anderson the author. When he had passed from thinking of men as slaves to the industrialism from which he had escaped, and had come to thinking of men and women as living in a world of primary experiences so vital that their inciting causes faded into unimportance, the factory lost interest as a factory and the slum as a slum, though they still might be used as backgrounds. The one matter that counted was to catch the rare moments when people were really living and to find the words that could record these moments.

And these rare moments were the moments when individuals were able to surmount or penetrate or break down the walls by which they were cut off from their fellows. The metaphor, once noted, recurs insistently throughout the stories. The wall, the wall, the wall. Only now and again do humans come into each other's spiritual presences. Partners, plotters, husbands, and wives are all held apart by impalpable barriers. "Men had themselves built the walls and now stood behind them, knowing dimly that beyond the walls there was warmth, light, air, beauty, life in fact—while at the same time and because of a kind of madness in themselves, the walls were constantly being built higher and stronger." In a sketch called "The Man's Story" the story-teller expounds this in prose and puts it into verse in a poem which ends,

Do you see this hand? Suppose it held a knife that could cut down through all the falseness in you. Suppose it could cut down through the sides of buildings and houses where thousands of people now lie asleep.

It would be something worth thinking about if the fingers of this hand gripped a knife that could cut and rip through all the ugly husks in which millions of lives are enclosed.

Elsewhere he alludes and realludes to the wall as a constant in all his observations on men and women.

IV

Let him change the metaphor. Enough has been said, perhaps too much, about materials. As to his processes, he has become "a word fellow"; words are his brothers; they have delivered him from thralldom; now he will serve them all the rest of his life. Nothing intrigues him so much as a pile of white paper on which he can scribble the words that want to be inscribed. Often they are the inevitable words; but now and then they are like that "scribble"; either they fail to give to the reader what they mean to the "word fellow" or he does not mean what he says. Perhaps what he wants here is to use a word of affectionate familiarity, as the Briton does when he calls his wife "old thing." But the usual suggestion of scribble is one of indifference and contempt. The "word fellow" cannot mean this or how could he write: "The result of the scribbling, the tale of perfect balance, all the elements of the tale understood, an infinite number of adjustments perfectly made, the power of self-criticism fully at work, the shifting surface of word values and color in full play, form and the rhythmic flow of thought and mood marching forward with the sentences—these are the things of a dream, of a far dim day toward which one goes knowing one can never arrive but infinitely glad to be on the road."

It is a marked fact about Sherwood Anderson's prose style that you close a book feeling that on the whole you have been reading poetry—that you have been through a variety of experiences with him and that some of them have been homely and some ugly and some very beautiful. You remember perhaps in a definite way certain passages that jarred, and you remember that probably or certainly he wanted to jar you by them. And you recall others that you deplore on grounds of taste—taste either in style or in subject—because you can see no special reason for the thing that he undertook to do. You realize all the while that in his later books he does one thing—he pursues the minds of his characters, finds out what thoughts, relevant or irrelevant, the stream of events arouses in them, and then expresses these thoughts in the idiom of the people whom they are invading; for after all, while we may feel in thrills or glows or raspings, we think in words and phrases. Always he has the dramatist's approach to his men and women, expressing them in their own ways. So you condone or accept or admire his method and you call it "sympathetic interpretation" or something of the sort, when he deals with the rough or vulgar character. Yet at the same time there persists the feeling that you have been reading poetry interspersed with passages of sheer beauty, passages that can be located and labeled like the passages that you have deplored.

In his recording, then, of "pure, crude fact,/ Secreted from man's life when hearts beat hard,/ And brains high-blooded, tick," crudity is sometimes consciously in the ascendant. Here is a young vagrant in New Orleans rooming-house in the half-dream of first awakening:

"You get a cup of such coffee for five cents and a big roll of bread. No swill. In Chicago, morning coffee at cheap places is like swill. Niggers like good things. Good big sweet words, flesh, corn, cane. Niggers like a free throat for song. You're a nigger down South and you get some white blood in you. A little more, and a little more. Northern travelers help, they say. Oh, Lord! Oh, my banjo dog!"

That is a lyric of a sort, but here is one of another sort on the same subject:

"Word-lovers, sound-lovers—the blacks seemed to hold a tone in some warm place, under their red tongues, perhaps. Their thick black lips were walls under which the tones hid . . . . the words coming from the throats of the black workers could not be understood by the boy but were strong and lovely. Afterwards when he thought of that moment Bruce always remembered the singing voices of the negro deck-hands as colors. Streaming reds, browns, golden yellows coming out of black throats. . . . . There were strange words about a 'banjo dog.' What was a 'banjo dog'? 'Ah, my banjo dog! Oh, oh! Oh, oh! Ah, my banjo dog!' "

And here is one of the second sort on a different subject:

"In old gardens in Europe and in some American places, where there are trees and thick bushes, a certain effect is achieved by setting small white figures on columns among the deep foliage, and Aline in fancy metamorphosed herself into such a white, dainty figure. She was a stone woman leaning over to raise to her arms a small child who stood with upraised hands, or she was a nun in the garden of a convent pressing a cross against her breast. As such a tiny stone figure she had no thoughts, no feelings. What she achieved was a kind of occasional loveliness among the dark night foliage of the garden."

Yet one has only to hunt for such passages as the latter two, or to quote them, to prove that the essential quality of Mr. Anderson's prose cannot be isolated in this way. It could only be illustrated in excerpts long enough to give evidence of its pervasive energy and its mobile flexibility. It is a medium for that sort of American life to which he was born and to which he is devoting himself. This is far from all of America, and it is part of America whose fineness is crudely articulated and largely devoid of nice nuances of manner. There are other writers for those who are not interested in this raw material. But in his treatment of it Sherwood Anderson in each succeeding book is better fulfilling his hope to make "his true note as an individual ring out above the hubbub of voices and then . . . . to use the strength and virility within himself to carry his word far."

CHAPTER IX
Sinclair Lewis

IN A generous burst of enthusiasm for the work of a fellow-novelist, Sinclair Lewis has told of what he most admires in a novel—of the kind of novel that he would most like to write. It is a splendid ideal that he holds up to view, finer than the novel which inspired him to put it into words, and finer than any he has written himself; though this latter is inevitable, for no artist has ever more than half expressed the fulness of his dreams. Dos Passos' *Manhattan Transfer* is the occasion of his utterance, but the cause of it lies deeper in his artist-self. He has written of the ideal novel and the ideal novelist; and what he has written—partly paraphrased and mostly quoted—comes to this:

The ideal novel—what may be the foundation of a whole school of novel-writing—will do what all novelists have frequently proven could not be done, will give the panorama, the soul, of a whole community. It will be full of the passion for the beauty and stir of life—of people, of rivers, and little hills and tall towers by dawn and furnace-kindled dusk.

Many wise persons will call such a novel sordid. But it will not be. For Keats himself felt no more passionate and sensitive reaction to beauty in her every guise than will inform it. It will not be expressed in terms of breakfast-food, easy for the moron to digest; nor in suave couplets, nor in descriptions of skyscrapers so neat that the real estate sections of the Sunday newspapers will beg to reprint them. It will deal not in photography but in broken color.

It will give the town, smell of it, sound of it, harsh and stirring sight of it; the churn and crunch of littered water between ferry-bow and slip; the midnight of skyscrapers where a dot of yellow betrays an illicit love or a weary accountant; insane clamor of subways in the dark; taste of spring in the law-haunted park; shriek of cabarets and howl of loneliness in hall-bedrooms—a thousand divinations of beauty without a touch of arty beauty-mongering. Naturally it will be free of that sickly complex whereby one hates the lyrical, the charming, the demure aspect of beauty, and perversely proclaims ugliness as alone noble; that natural yet also puerile revolution against the prettifying of the machine-made manufacturing of commercial tales. Yes, this novelist will be slated as sordid, a low fellow. He will not see life as necessarily approaching the ideals of a Hartford insurance agent. He will see it as a roaring, thundering, incalculable, obscene, magnificent glory.

II

Mr. Lewis has not yet written a novel of th
sort; it is quite doubtful whether anyone else ha
but the direction of his work has been an approach
toward this, and because he has traveled so far; because there was so little to suggest in his earlier
books that he might even set his face toward such a
goal, the thing that he has done in *Main Street* and
Babbitt and *Arrowsmith* has been a promise as well as
a performance. He began with *Our Mr. Wrenn*, a
book which was as modest and unimpressive as its
central character. Mr. Wrenn is a nobody of the
business world, faithful, biddable, with a spark of
romance in him which makes him yearn for the
grand adventure of travel. A little legacy gives him
the chance which he seizes by going to England on
a cattle boat, tarrying uneasily a few weeks, and
scurrying back to the big city and his job. The only
thing that happens to him is a thing that might
have happened to someone but could never have
happened to such as he, when he falls in with an
alluring, sophisticated bohemian dabbler in the
arts and interests her enough to become a plaything
of a little longer than the moment. Then New York
again, a new boarding-house, emancipation from a
harridan landlady, a meeting with the inevitable
She, a momentary re-encounter with the titian dabbler, and a wrenlike domesticity to which he is con-
signed as he hurries home through the brisk autumn
breeze beneath a sunset that no longer allures him

o wander, with seven cents' worth of potato salad
nd the prospect of the evening paper and a game of
nochle with Nellie. It is a long way from him
to any "roaring, thundering, incalculable, obscene,
magnificent glory."

The Trail of the Hawk is another very youthful
book, but very much more vigorous. And it introduces several characters who are to reappear with
different names. Carl Ericson has the makings of
Martin Arrowsmith. His Ruth is a forerunner of
Joyce Lanyon. Bone Stillman, village atheist, is a
preincarnation of Miles Bjornstam. It is the tale of
a stormy petrel rather than a hawk, who marries, as
Mr. Lewis likes to marry his men, a lady who cares
more for the amenities than he does, but more for
him than for the amenities. It tells of their love-
makings and tiffs and reconciliations, and in the last
chapter sends them to sea on an indeterminate vaga-
bondage, he quoting Kipling and she speculating on
the possibility of a Society for the Spread of Madness among the Respectable. On the whole, it is a
rather engaging novel. It is built around a real character, with some slight capacities to roar and
thunder, with a tinge of the hobo, a strain of virgin-
ity, a flair for adventure, and a hanker for taking
risks; one of the type who by the hundred were soon
to flock to the first Officer's Training Camps, and to
find themselves, for a while at least, in a life which
was measured by something more challenging than
a time-clock routine. As a social chameleon he is

a little out of character, for he is as quick as a girl in taking on the protective coloration of the best people, when he does not forget himself; and he develops what collegians call a "line" of pseudo-clever talk which his author seems to enjoy as much as he does though it could hardly intrigue any but post-adolescent readers. Much more significant than this is the bromidic conversation of secondary figures which was to feature so largely in the later stories.

With two books behind him Mr. Lewis did not hurry. It was two years later when *The Job* appeared, presenting the city at closer range and more nearly as his ideal novelist would present it. In these two years Mr. Lewis' mind became—in the slang phrase of pedagogy—"socialized." He had discovered what pedagoguese would term two phenomena—the Social Order and Woman-in-Business. Una Golden, without knowing it at the start, is a modernist. She has seen through the futility of the male sex in terms of her father and her elderly suitor of Panama, Pennsylvania. She advances on Manhattan, learns typewriting and stenography, gets a succession of jobs, finds out the drabness and the pettiness of the business system, and, for a moment, the almost beautiful thing that business can be. She marries a bounder, is eventually freed from him, starts anew, develops an ability to plan and perform, creates a real job of her own, and then finds again the one man who has ever deeply appealed to her. It is a novel with a solution; for the Woman-in-Business comes into her own when life allows her to retain her job and gives her a baby to boot. The idiom is an unhappy one, and the story ends too soon. More exactly, life promises her a baby to neglect.

The Job is a more convincing piece of work than the two novels that preceded it, and, for that matter, than the two negligible stories that followed: *The Innocents* and *Free Air*. Mr. Lewis is not primarily a story-teller; he is an expositor who uses the narrative form. To follow an individual through his experiences as one would follow and observe a force in nature, to see him always as an individual and yet to see in him the human elements which are timeless—this is neither his interest nor his gift. To Mr. Lewis, thus far in his career, a story if it has any power must serve not merely as a story but also as a vehicle. Life for him is not inherent in John Smith or Babbitt. It is the force that surrounds the man. In applauding his fellow-novelist he applauds him not for creating characters, but for painting the panorama of the metropolis. Of Zenith he writes, "Vast is the power of cities to reclaim the wanderer. More than mountains or the shore-devouring sea, a city retains its character, imperturbable, cynical, holding behind apparent changes its essential purpose." It is small wonder in the circumstances, that with one exception he has not made a character strong enough to dominate the stories of which they are only incidental features. Una Golden is not this character. She is singularly colorless even in her success, though as a type she is significant as one of an endless procession of women marching down the Main streets, expressing their discontent with life as they find it and vaguely asserting their right to make something vaguely different from it. The city is in this book, and an idea is in it, and, more important than these, satire for the first time asserts itself effectively. He has arrived at his own manner when, for example, he writes of Pemberton's: "It has been calculated that ninety-three million women in all parts of the world have ruined their complexions, and therefore, their souls, by Pemberton's creams and lotions for saving the same; and that nearly three-tenths of the alcohol consumed in prohibition counties is obtained in Pemberton's tonics and blood-builders and women's specifics, these last being regarded by large farmers with beards as especially tasty and stimulating. Mr. Pemberton is the Napoleon of patent medicine, and also the Napoleon of drugs used by physicians to cure the effects of patent medicines. He is the Shakespeare of ice-cream sodas, and the Edison of hot-water bags."

If the chronicle were to move in perfect order, the next step to record would be Mr. Lewis' advance on the city; but his next attempt in fact was to picture the heart and mind of America. Wiseacres had been saying for a generation that the time had passed for the writing of the American novel, that America was too far flung and heterogeneous for any such possible document. They had been saying it because they could not imagine a story that could include Tom Sawyer and Posson Jone and Uncle Remus and Colonel Carter and Silas Lapham and Rose of Dutcher's Coolly and William Sylvanus Baxter in the same company. And no such company could be imagined outside of fantasy. They lived too early. But a few ingenious men changed all that by the extensive use of wires and rails and gasoline and billboards.

There had been two literary—more or less literary—traditions of the American small town. One was that it remained "the one sure abode of friendship, honesty, and clean-sweet, marriageable girls." In story after story the American youth made his pilgrimage, had his fling, renounced the world and the sins of the metropolis, and returned to the village street, the white picket fence, the faithful family dog, the lilacs, the moonlight, and happiness ever after. It was Auburn, loveliest village of the plain, over and over again; but it wasn't America. The other tradition was that villages were chiefly characterized by "whiskers, iron dogs upon lawns, gold bricks, checkers, jars of gilded cat-tails, and shrewd, comic, old men, who are known as 'hicks,' and who ejaculate 'Waal, I swan!' " This village, too, had disappeared in the days of Silas Lapham and Colonel Carter.

The climax of civilization, said Mr. Lewis, is the town of today that "thinks not in hoss-swapping but in cheap motor-cars, telephones, ready-made clothes, silos, alfalfa, kodaks, phonographs, leather-upholstered Morris chairs, bridge prizes, oil stocks, motion-pictures, land-deals, unread sets of Mark Twain, and a chaste version of national politics." This provincial town with its standardization of mediocrity might be let alone, he thought, if it were merely passive; but "it has become a force seeking to dominate the earth, to drain the hills and the sea of color. . . . . Its conception of a community ideal is not the grand manner, the noble aspiration, the fine, aristocratic pride, but cheap labor for the kitchen and rapid increase in the price of land. . . . . If all the provincials were kindly there would be no reason for desiring the town to seek great traditions. It is the small busy men crushingly powerful in their common purpose, viewing themselves as men of the world but keeping themselves men of the cash-register and the comic film, who make the town a sterile oligarchy"; and who are subjecting the country to the domination of the fundamentalists, prohibitionists, hundred per cent Americans and go-getters.

As a thesis, and an indictment, this is clear enough, and there is plenty of evidence on which to establish it. It is not only sound in general but in particular it is reasonable in taking issue against the kind of standardization that results in obnoxious stupidity in contrast with the passive kindliness which may be stupid but which is for the most part harmless. Excellence in a thesis novel, however, requires excellence in the novel as well as in the thesis; and it requires incomparably good story-telling to carry the double pack. Mr. Lewis admits great admiration for Dickens, who could carry both burdens, and praises him, as who does not, for his creation of characters, but condemns him for dragging in pages of "lying hypocrisy." Mr. Lewis neither offends nor achieves with Dickens. *Main Street* pretty largely makes its case, as a case, but leaves in the memory no imperative episode and no unforgettable person. One comes with a touch of surprise to a passage which alludes to Champ Perry and Sam Clark as kindly and to Harry Haydock, Dave Dyer, and Jackson Elder as the malignants in the social group. To look back over the story is to find that the author is right, but, without the reminder and the review, they all belong to one indistinguishably vulgar and stupid crowd. The few people that one remembers are not essentially Main Streeters. Carol Kennicott is the Woman-out-of-Business, a foil and complement to Una Golden. Doc Kennicott, perhaps represents Gopher Prairie, but in the story he is used only to play up to the leading lady, though he is bigger than his rôle. One has vague memories of others, but cannot recall their names. . . . .

The creation of a character is, of course, what Mr. Lewis did achieve in *Babbitt*. The success of George F. as an artistic creation lies in the fact that he is not the caricature that he is often said to be.

He is sufficiently complicated to belong to the race of little people, who are usually more multiplex than the great ones of the earth, whose greatness is in their relative simplicity. And his failure as an individual lies in the pathetic fact that he actually does struggle to save his own soul and to free himself from the web of circumstance which is too much for him, but to which he is never completely resigned. He plans to go into the law until he finds a trusting brown head on his shoulder which considers itself engaged to him, and, lacking the brutality to disavow love, he marries and makes money in real estate. He inclines toward honesty, but an astute senior partner leads him into transactions that, lacking fight, he winks at. He wants to be faithful to his perfunctory marriage vows, but lacking backbone, he is bored into a shuffling intrigue with an alluring client. He would like to be something more than a timidly abusive standpatter, but, in the face of the gang of good fellows whose approval is the light of day to him, he cannot pay the price of social and business ostracism.

Always around him, overwhelming all but the last vestige of protest in him, is the city; a city of the potential splendors and roarings and thunderings that Mr. Lewis has not yet quite pictured. It reclaims him and standardizes him. The material side of it he likes; he flutters feebly against the standardization of thought. And in the end, irredeemably Babbitt, he still yearns for better luck for his son: "I've never done a single thing I wanted to in my whole life! I don't know's I've accomplished anything except just get along. I figure out I've made about a quarter of an inch out of a possible hundred rods. Well, maybe you'll carry on things further. I don't know. But I do get a kind of sneaking pleasure out of the fact that you knew what you wanted to do, and did it. Well these folks in there will try to bully you, and tame you down. Tell 'em to go to the devil. I'll back you. Take your factory job if you want to. Don't be scared of the family. No, nor all of Zenith. Nor of yourself, the way I've been.' Mrs. Wharton has used what Mr. Lewis might have adopted as a title, *The Custom of the Country;* but Mr. Lewis' title is better for this book, for it has to do with an indubitable character. In a measure it is true that Babbitt rode to fame down Main Street; but a populous street never yet more than gave the opportunity for an imposing procession, and Babbitt's progress was at the head of an innumerable army.

III

Martin Arrowsmith stands at the far intellectual pole from George F. Babbitt; yet he has the same history, and, granting the gifts with which he is endowed, he comes off very little better. The conventional story of the day has to do with the young genius who grows up in uncongenial surroundings, stifled now by poverty, now by mammon, now by dilettantism. Then he achieves as an artist and enjoys the spiritual satisfaction of turning up his nose at the world as he espouses poverty or marries wealth. Arrowsmith is a genius but a scientist. He has a conception of science which makes it one with art and religion. It makes a man uncontent with half-truth. The business game is a silly insufficiency to him, but no more so than what he regards as the unfounded pursuits of dreamy idealism. He is an intolerant, but he works for human welfare though he has little respect for most human beings. He does not expect intelligent sympathy; and he is ready to sacrifice. "In Martin Arrowsmith there were no decorative heroisms, no genius for amours, no exotic wit, no edifyingly borne misfortunes. He presented neither picturesque elegance nor a moral message. He was full of hasty faults and of a perverse honesty; a young man, often unkindly, often impolite. But he had one gift, a curiosity whereby he saw nothing as ordinary."

He is human enough, then, to be put into a story. The story which is told of him is a story of the scientist in conflict with his avowed allies. The vision is given him at the start by an old bacteriologist; but he loses it in the need of supporting a wife. For a while he is a Will Kennicott, a by-no-means-despicable country doctor. Then he is a health-department official in a western town where boosting for better babies is legitimate as long as the milk supply is left alone. The pictures of village and town life are quite as convincing as in the books devoted to them, and in Almus Pickerbaugh, medical demagogue and ultimate Congressman, there is an almost Dickensian finality. Then Lewis and Arrowsmith together invade New York City and the same thing happens to them that happened to the young crusader when he first fell in with preventive medicine. "Everything became clear to Martin—too clear."

These two young men descend on the metropolis armed with a deadly thesis. They are prepared to demonstrate that inhospitable as the countryside is to the fine enthusiasms of the scientist, the great city is more dangerous. The country is stupid, but the city, with its show of friendliness, is subtly and insidiously dangerous. It offers the scientific investigator a laboratory and assistance and a living wage, but it begrudges him the time to follow his curiosity to its final goal, to be certain of his findings, to be deliberate and modest in his statement of results. According to this thesis the control of the great research foundation inevitably falls into the hands of men who are managers, exploiters, publicity-seekers. To yield to them is to compromise with the devil. To take up with the fashionable patrons of good works is to enter the purgatory especially devised for the objects of polite patronage. To oppose them is to risk not merely personal success, but to put in jeopardy the fine ends to which the scientist is dedicated. To place a genuine devotee of the truth in such a position is either to break him or to banish him.

This is a striking proposition, and there is a good deal of reason for maintaining it. The man who knows of philistinism in the medical world has no quarrel with Mr. Lewis on the score of his truthfulness. Some of the sources of his character studies are recognizable, the rest, with the exception of Tubbs the exploiter, are well above the level of caricature. But the story falters in two respects. The lesser is the result of attempting to put unfamiliar and technical material into a story-fable. The great crisis in Arrowsmith's career arises when he is in charge of a plague fight in the West Indies, and when he has to decide between using his serum to save life as he may, or using it selectively to make a final demonstration of its effectiveness. Circumstance seems to force him to the former course; though in sober fact, unless he had a regiment of assistants and tuns of serum, his widest use could never reach the whole population. His problem of selection was automatically solved for him. The major weakness arises from his insistence on the thesis. He tells the truth but not the whole truth about the medical world. Pasteur, facing every obstacle, fought the French government to a finish—and won. If America is arraigned as being less corrigible, there can be cited American men in medical research who have not compounded with principle, who are free agents in full career with abounding honors and troops of friends. There is no hint of such a figure in the fable; yet Arrowsmith's retreat to the hills is recorded as inevitable not only to his nature but also to the nature of the situation. It was inevitable for him only because he was an unheroic figure.

Now, latest of all, comes *Elmer Gantry*, an up-to-date picaresque novel. The central figure is a rogue and a bounder who chooses the ministry for his calling because he is bred for it, evangelized into it, and finds in it an outlet for part of his emotions and for all of his overpowering love of self-display. Ousted from his first Baptist connection, but not unfrocked, he does well in commercial salesmanship until he falls under the spell of a woman evangelist as whose assistant he comes nearest to decency because of his personal devotion. In fact, she is so commanding a figure that the author has to invoke a holocaust to get her out of the story—an obvious and desperate device, for Gantry's soul must not be saved, and he is in imminent peril of salvation. After a venture in New Thought from which he is discharged for pilfering from his prophetess, he finds an opening in Methodism in which he progresses through increasingly remunerative pastorates, irredeemably corrupt and headed toward a bishopric on the way to even greater conquest as the story ends.

Elmer Gantry is Mr. Lewis' first attempt at a rake's progress, the point of which, as a narrative genre, is that the rake is not a unique character but a typical product of the social order. His progress is a series of intrigues, all but one of them shabby, with Juanita, with the daughter of a nearby farmer, a willing choir-singer, a chambermaid at Solomon Junction, with Lulu Bains, with Sharon Falconer, with Lulu again, with a Chautauqua "talent," and finally with an adventuress who in order to save her own skin refrains from ruining him by public exposure. He has a punch which he resorts to against three successive hecklers at meetings interspersed along his career and against a spindling bootlegger on a sensational raid. And in his own parlance he has a "punch" in the pulpit which depends on the same physique and voice and abounding vigor that intrigues women and wins him an election to the Rotary Club.

He is a timely figure, and in his timeliness he is likely to achieve a smashing *succès de scandal* for his author; greater than the success of *Arrowsmith*, for a hundred entertain a personal feeling for religion to every one who harbors any loyalty to abstract science. But Gantry's timeliness makes him and the book about him a contribution to journalism rather than to literature. He is, like Martin Arrowsmith, a proponent for a thesis, and like Arrowsmith again he is the proponent of a thesis with which the author has acquainted himself through deliberate gathering of the material more than through the intimate knowledge that arises from experience and unconscious observation. He pictures in detail the evangelical life of twenty years ago but he fails to realize it with the fulness of either Anne Parrish's recollections in *The Perennial Bachelor* or Edna Ferber's researches in *Show Boat*. Mrs. Stowe, Mrs. Deland, Mrs. Humphry Ward, had lived the ecclesiastical life of which they wrote in *Oldtown Folks*, *John Ward, Preacher*, and *Robert Elsmere*. Mr. Lewis' study is as obvious as Mr. Churchill's in *The Inside of the Cup*. He has no intimate feeling for religion.

In the attack on his thesis Mr. Lewis attempts to write a story about an individual and to draw up an indictment of an institution. These two tasks could be one if the career of Elmer Gantry were actually an indictment of religion and the church. But this is not the fact. Gantry is not a product of the church; he is the product of a philistine and stupid social order which makes it possible for him to exploit the church without ever in any real sense belonging to it. And Mr. Lewis evidently half-recognizes the failure of his narrative to carry its own burden by his interpolation of long and dispensable dialogues between decent and intelligent parsons to whom the priestly rogue is absolutely alien in manners, morals, and mind.

What they have to say is interesting as a formulation of an indictment against the teachings of the divinity schools, the ministry, the Protestant denominations, Catholicism, and Christianity as a whole. The only conclusion to be drawn is that in Mr. Lewis' opinion the unprejudiced observer can find little to say for any of them. That is an interesting opinion, and no doubt the debate will be continued far beyond the limits of his book. But it could be withdrawn, with all its elaborations, without in the slightest way affecting the story except by relieving it of a dead weight of material which is suggested by the central character but irrelevant to it.

IV

Among the many definitions of literature the one that declares it to be a criticism of life is by no means the least acceptable; but in any form of literature besides the essay it is an essential feature that it be conveyed in definite objects, people, scenes, events, and that anything of truth and anything of criticism be conveyed implicitly in these as truth is conveyed in life, without exposition from the creator. In his admiring commentary on Mr. Dos Passos, Mr. Lewis writes on this assumption. The ideal novel will not be easy to understand; in its faithfulness to life it will be incalculable. In the major stories which earned him his fame Mr. Lewis in a measure lived up to this assumption. It is fair to say that *Main Street* is not the easiest of stories to understand; it is perfectly safe to say that *Babbitt* has been quite misunderstood by the vast majority of readers. But in turning away from these two criticisms of life Mr. Lewis turned to criticisms of institutions—from the soul of a whole community to single organizations and their besetting faults. In doing which he began to document and argue and harangue. It is an experi-

ence almost exactly the reverse of Mr. Anderson's
in the same years, and in this contrast the advantage is indubitably with Mr. Anderson in so far as
art is to be taken into the reckoning.

As Mr. Lewis knows what art is, showing this
in both criticism and creation, some experience,
either in life or in reading, may lead him back toward his ideal. He has a long reach of activity ahead
of him. Possibly before he takes this turn he will
have to vent himself, like the unctuous resident of
the Third Floor Back, on all the other inmates in
his boarding-house—the bench and the legislature,
finance and industry. At present he is indicting certain aspects of American life with the zest of a
state's attorney intent on making a reputation by
piling up convictions, but while he is at it he is
falling under his own condemnation of surrendering
to "the sickly complex whereby one hates the
lyrical, the charming, the demure aspect of beauty,
and perversely proclaims ugliness." In theory and
in practice he has shown that he is capable of more
than this.

CHAPTER X
Democracy and Public Taste

ONE day not long ago I was dining with some English friends in California. We were on American soil but under an English roof, so that for the moment I was an alien among Britons—they had me three to one. With that frankness which is one of their engaging traits, and apparently with their guest as their cue, they began without loss of time to dilate on the cultural shortcomings of America. The movies, the follies, the fiction magazines! woman's clubs, chautauquas, cheap evangelism!! prohibition, jazz!!! The waves of assault poured in while I was mobilizing for defense. Finally I found an opening for the edge of word.

"*Imprimis*"; I said, "supposing these things are so, what about the English? I don't seem to remember an embargo on these American products. And, *secundo;* if you could dictate, how would you meet the situation 'out here,' you who are so complacently 'in'? I'll concede you some of your charges but I won't grant that movies, woman's clubs, chautauquas, and jazz are supplements to the seven deadly sins."

I had rather to press the points, but after an hour or so they had penetrated the not too thin skins of my host and his countrymen. Then they capitulated handsomely.

"Of course," they said cheerily, "if you take that line we might as well admit that we raise merry hell with England too when we are at home."

I pleased them with the assurance that they knew how to, and they replied that if they didn't it wasn't for lack of practice; and as the conversation then took an economic turn with a newly entered American who was more than able to hold his own, I made use of the breathing spell to recognize that they were only engaged in a diverting indoor game. "We have done . . . . ," they intoned, "and you have left undone . . . . and there is no help in us." But they had not meant it at table any more than they mean it in the pew. It was all in a manner of speaking. They were like the upholsterer's widow in *The Citizen of the World*, who could not bear to be caught enjoying anything at Vauxhall and was happy only when she was deepest in "miserable refinement." Yet that is not quite fair; for they were gaily devastating and we were all the happier for the set-to.

No doubt there is more to be gained from discussing the contrasting cultures of neighboring nations than there is in fighting over their conflicting patriotisms, in the exchange of a book of poems for a labor-saving invention than in the purchase of a hundred square miles for a hundred thousand slain;

but for people, or for peoples, who have contracted the habit of self-criticism the temptation is evidently very strong to make the indictment as damning as possible and in drawing comparisons to pick out Main Street rather than Fifth Avenue for contrast with the Avenue de l'Opéra.

If comparisons must be made, and there is no denying that their effects are often wholesome, there is another way of drawing them: by going to the past instead of to the East. (It is typical of the stonewall tradition Columbus encountered that the American is even yet supposed to look three quarters round the globe to the land of the rising sun, though he actually goes east to the Occident and west to the Orient.) It has been done, of course, and the unsentimental and uncompromising truth-teller has come up from his dive into the remote depths with his bag full of the usual scarifying conclusions. There is such a miscellany on the bottom of the sea that one can find about what one is looking for, just as he can in the flotsam and jetsam on the surface.

II

If one is to think to any purpose about popular taste, I take it that the thinking will not be limited to negations. There has never been a time in America without a perceptible interest in architecture, literature, music, nor a time since the first Independence Day when the interest was not traceable in painting, sculpture, and the theater. But there has never been a time of equal interest in all of them. The more widely popular likings are limited to the indispensable and the inexpensive. People must have houses for themselves and for the uses of the community; these are mute and lasting records of popular taste. Tunefulness is irrepressible and widespread and recordable. Books and magazines cost something, but not very much. The theaters are a mild extravagance, and should be estimated in terms of their qualities as well as the extent of their public. Painting and sculpture are farthest from general reach and general possession.

The century and a half from the first Virginia and Massachusetts settlements to the Battle of Concord and the Fourth of July of the next year makes a long story; but when it is told the Americans of the new nation that was conceived in liberty knew less than nothing about liberty of taste. In the first burst of national self-consciousness the most that a prophet like John Trumbull could hope was that America would follow English models well enough to have a home-bred Milton, Addison, Pope, Thomson, Swift, and Young, and rise to so dizzy a climax that some Shakespeare here should charm the rising stage, while

> A second Watts shall strike the heavenly lyre
> And other muses other bards inspire.

Richardson was the favorite novelist, and the native story-tellers, mostly women, followed and surpassed him in sentimentalism. A third of all the stage productions were Shakespeare, another third were post-Restoration Englishmen, and when Royall Tyler prologued his "Contrast" and William Dunlap his "André" with patriotic allusions to their native themes they had said all there was to say on the American quality of their wares, for the homespun had been carefully and obviously cut to English measure. There was some good painting done in those days by West and Stuart and Copley, all learned from English masters. There was some charming architecture—churches after Wren and Inigo Jones and dwellings in excellent Georgian style. And the music, religious and secular, had the same origin for the most part: "America," as everyone knows; "The Star-Spangled Banner," a new set of words to a London drinking song that had already had forty variants; "Yankee Doodle" from an English ballad tune; "Home, Sweet Home," from a Sicilian folk theme. The one lasting song from the period that began in America, Fyle's march adapted for "Hail, Columbia," was Handelian, charmingly so, in every detail.

All of which is a way of saying that the established taste of America in the early days of the Republic was English taste and for the most part very good taste. And it was anything but democratic in its origins. It was born of a courtly tradition. Timothy Dwight, thrilled with a sense of epic possibilities, wrote a poem on the present and future of America in terms of a Connecticut town. The subject matter was local and the sentiments anti-British. The gateway to the millennium was in the Western World. Yet when he undertook "Greenfield Hill" he planned, he said, to imitate, in the several parts, the manner of as many British poets, and he did not carry the plan all the way through simply because of the trouble. Tyler filled "The Contrast" with noble American sentiments, but wrote as nearly as possible in the manner of Farquhar and Sheridan, used his home-spun American villager as a comic relief character, and could not resist making fun of his own grandiloquent hero. Joseph Hopkinson chanted "Let independence be our boast,/Ever mindful what it cost," but in fitting his verse to a courtly melody, he was a gentleman of the old school essaying the rôle of the American braggart. Irving and his collaborators did *The Salmagundi Papers* after Goldsmith; *The Sketch Book* was an Addisonian aftermath. Thomas Jefferson prevailed with difficulty on his state legislature to build the capitol in Richmond on the lines of the Maison Carrée, and did the plant for the University of Virginia according to strict classical canons. From 1770 when Freneau and Brackenridge spouted their commencement colloquy on "The Rising Glory of America" there followed a succession of appeals for a native American art and culture. Yet seventy years later Longfellow, even after he had written that the "national ballad is a virgin soil in New England," took the position that "a national literature is the expression of national character and thought; and as our character and modes of thought do not differ essentially from those of England, our literature cannot."

Three years earlier Emerson had borne witness to this by his appeal, in "The American Scholar," for some independence of American thought. Edwin Forrest's attempts to encourage an American drama by rewarding plays on primitive American characters had elicited a couple of prize-winning Indian tales and then *The Broker of Bogota* and *Jack Cade* and *Spartacus the Gladiator*. The poets of the eighteen forties were writing "poems distilled from foreign poems" according to Whitman's later verdict. There was the beginning of an American art colony in Italy. There was an increasing flow of university students to France and Germany. Longfellow was right about the cultivated Americans with whom he was acquainted. Their tastes had changed but little in the two generations since the Revolutionary War. They liked courtly things and behaved in courtly ways. They were the men of whom Dickens could write on his first visit to America that they were "gentlemen . . . . who would shed a grace upon, and do honor to, any society in the civilized world."

III

But the Americans among whom Longfellow achieved his wide popularity with his ballads and psalms and household lyrics and simple narratives were people of a very different stamp. "I have a great notion," he wrote once, "of working on the *people's* feelings," supplying his own italics. He succeeded in doing it, just as Jefferson succeeded in establishing a tradition of democracy, though neither Longfellow nor Jefferson were shoulder-rubbing democrats. The on-coming generation, according to its own testimony, included an ominous element who were as untutored as the English yokel and a hundred times more assertive. They ran the country newspapers, counted the country vote, represented "up-state" or "down-state" constituencies in local and national politics, supplied party spoils to their own kind, and in the towns developed into annoying parvenus by dint of shrewdness and hard work. Their only interest in any aristocratic tradition was to overthrow it—its power, its manners, its predilections. They were the progenitors of the modern hundred per cent American, and like their descendants they were long on shouting for democracy and utterly intolerant of freedom of opinion, freedom of speech, and individual liberty. Condemn them as harshly as feeling and vocabulary will allow, Cooper went further with short and ugly words, and Whittier and Lowell and Thoreau and Holmes deeper in caustic scorn.

Between the gentlemen who would grace any court and the "shirt-sleeved Charlemagne of Empires new,/Who meeting Caesar's self would slap his back,/Call him 'Old Horse' and challenge to a drink," was a great body of quiet, self-respecting, and respectable citizens who were all unconscious of acknowledging traditions or exercising taste. Yet they did both, and in the older communities were as distinctly the products of their neighborhoods as the oaks and elms and maples that shaded their roadsides. I think of a modest New England town on the outskirts of which I have summered for years. It is a town for the most part of white clapboards and green shutters, and as far as it can be told in those two details, the history of American domestic architecture is told in its dwellings. No one with the least sense for line and proportion can mistake a modern house there for an old one. This is not merely true of the King's Grant mansion which went up in the seventeenth century, and the few other monuments from the remoter past; it applies to the houses that represent the Revolution and the early Republic, and that may be in perfect repair today. They have an ease and a dignity in the set of their roofs, a harmony of proportion, a grace that depends on neither curve nor decoration. And yet when you inquire as to actual dates you find now and then a surprise. There is a modest little one just down the road put up by the father of the elderly villager who is living in it today. The father did it with his own hands. There was no architect involved; but it is a perfect thing, for the father was so completely heir to a sound tradition that he saw no other way than this right way of handling line and mass and proportion. He knew it just as he knew the Doxology and the Twenty-third Psalm.

Yet in this and neighboring towns there are dwellings much more ambitious in scale, built after 1825 by men not so thoroughly in the tradition, which betray the decadence of their periods first by a loss in simplicity, then by pretentiousness, and later still by fussiness and flimsiness. And in the newer parts of the country and the encircling new districts in the growing cities, frame buildings erected without aid or interference of the architect are bleak and angular, or specious with false fronts and tawdry decoration. In these latter years there has been an extraordinary recovery in both domestic and public architecture in America; but in the middle of the nineteenth century something was gone; something was happening.

The same thing was gone, and the same thing was happening to music and particularly to church music. The original opposition to melodious singing and to instrumental music in the churches was overcome a long time before the Revolution. The objections among the non-conformists had been that any concession to beauty was a concession either to paganism or to the corrupt traditions of the Church of Rome or the Church of England. Yet in time musical instruments and musical singing had taken the place of the dreary lining out of psalms. Under the new order the first hymn words continued to be simple paraphrases from the Bible and the first hymn tunes had the simple dignity that belonged to the chorales of the older churches. The democratic non-conformists were doing with their worship what they had already done with their meeting-houses in following the patterns supplied from an aristocratic past. But the same things happened to hymns as to buildings. The worshipers covered the serene interiors of their Colonial chapels with stenciled frescoes, or abandoned them altogether for what Lowell called "Gothic contract shams"; and they substituted sentimental waltz melodies for the fine austerity of the older four-four chants. It was a transition from Addison's "The spacious firmament on high" by way of Holmes's "Lord of all being, throned afar" to Miss Lathbury's "Day is dying in the west"; and though the latter has the values of its kind, it marks the transition from Handel and Haydn to Moody and Sankey. In the meanwhile the old choirs recruited from the congregations were replaced by hired quartets who frescoed the services with Gounod and Rossini, just as the decorators had frescoed the walls and ceilings, with fancy ornamentations that had no basic relation to the compositions they embellished. Only Catholic and Episcopal services maintained their solid traditions. For the rest democracy adopted as accessories paid entertainers, ungowned, with exhibits of the latest millinery and haberdashery, to sing florid pieces and lead the congregations in sentimental lyrics.

It is time to slow down a little, for the inclination is all too strong in any scenic ride down the decades to jam the cap over the eyes, grip the sides of the car, and whoop for sheer delight in the speed. For intellectual or aesthetic purposes the ride ceases to be scenic and might just as well be a drop down a mine shaft. To keep the eyes open and to put on the brakes is to recognize all sorts of exceptional and palliative facts overlooked by casual shoot-the-chuters. Thus, there was occasional good domestic architecture in the United States between 1840 and 1900 in spite of the decline into the abyss of the Queen Anne period. Where old residences survived and the neighborhoods did not decline, their influence survived in some measure with them. Or again, Moody and Sankey affected the Bible school and the young people's meeting more than they did the Sunday-morning service. (Quite so! And so much the worse!) And as for American song-writers there were some, particularly secular composers like George Root and Dan Emmett, who were positive, vigorous, and quite home-bred in their quality. Moreover, the whole story is not to be told in terms of only two popular arts. It is best to be traced through the arts which have had the widest response and the widest personal expression; but in the arts which are enjoyed by patronage rather than by participation and which have enjoyed a growing and changing patronage, the characters are the same and the plot is not essentially different.

Life and nature are seldom so simple as any generalization would make them. Yet the Rocky Mountains, for all their peaks over fourteen thousand feet high, have a discoverable average level; and so does any human generation. Granting the peaks and valleys, the popular taste of the mid-century in the United States was nearer the valley than the peaks. The frankly imposed and frankly accepted domination of the gentry was passed. The shadow of Andrew Jackson lay between the present and the dimming figures of Washington and Jefferson. Jefferson had been devoted to his violin and his draughting board and to the people. The people were in power, but they remembered his political faith and cared nothing for his aesthetics. Until they should develop tastes of their own to replace those they had discarded they were bound to wander in the wilderness. And they are not out of it yet.

IV

Such is the story of the American theater. Washington, courtly Virginian, was an enthusiastic patron. In his day and up to 1825 the stage was completely dominated by the English, in spite of a four-year fad for German adaptations, chiefly Dunlap's, and a less sensational use of French plays, chiefly by Payne. There were fifty years of professional stock companies, and twenty-five of visiting stars who came over with their costumes and their lines and played with what support they could find in the cities they visited. Their rôles were in plays that had succeeded in London. From the outset a drama-starved American public patronized with something near to avidity the rather high level of drama that was offered them: Shakespeare, Dryden, Otway, Congreve, Farquhar, Addison, Steele, and in time Goldsmith and Sheridan and Cumberland and the Colmans, and stage versions of Scott and Byron. A score or two of the successful American productions were modeled after these.

Then when a kind of dramatic saturation point had been reached, so that mere entrance to the enchanted theater was not enough, patronage lagged until it was stimulated by spectacular plays and equestrian plays and child actors and operettas with *entr'actes* of sword dances and egg dances and tightrope walking and song hits. Still, however, the favorite old plays could prevail in the hands of recognized stars. Any man with a name could swing round the circuit annually on a repertory of a half-dozen Shakespeare plays and *Venice Preserved* and *A New Way to Pay Old Debts* and *The Iron Chest* and *Brutus* and *Virginius*. The tradition was British and the best actors and actresses. It was then that the Jeffersons and Booths, the Hacketts, Sotherns, and Barrymores established their lines in America, and that the Keans and Macready and the Kembles made their frequent rounds. As American play-making asserted itself the Yankee character was developed and the comic negro (successor to the stage Irishman and the stage Jew) and then the whole vast "Ethiopian drama," and the minstrel show with its now almost forgotten vogue. As American producers came to the fore the dominance of the English tradition was for the first time effectively challenged. America and all of Europe contributed to a cosmopolitan repertory, and, with the appeals to the populace broadened and multiplied, over the American stage rose the shadow of the nonpareil of showmen, P. T. Barnum. It was he and his like who once for all established the distinction between the playgoer and the showgoer in the United States. It was not in fact a new distinction, but it did not become a vital distinction until the theater was sold to the show-goers who have ruled it through the box office ever since. This is nothing to go into heroics over, but it is something to recognize more clearly than is usually done.

Most of the mournful and undiscriminating talk current about the American theater of today is based on the mistaken assumption that it is a mysterious institution with a single, clear identity. But it is not. The lowest terms to which dramatic activity in America can be reduced are two—and this is desperately forcing the issue—the commercial theater and the art theater. The art theater—the qualifying word is unsatisfactory, but it is hard to find a better—is conducted primarily for the presentation of good plays and intelligent acting. It has to pay for itself, for it has never been generally underwritten as the opera and the orchestra have always been, and it has to depend for its support on an artistic and intelligent body of playgoers. There are as many of these now, probably as high a percentage of them, as there ever were in the United States. But they feel no single-minded devotion to good drama. They are at best potential supporters of good plays and good acting, if they happen to know about the good plays, and happen to have free evenings to see them in, and happen not to be lured away by a rival show when the time comes for buying the seats.

The nearest thing to any impressive mobilization of this constituency is the New York Theater Guild, which in its short life has enjoyed and deserved almost unparalleled success. A thousand little, or neighborhood, or workshop, or community theaters from Provincetown to Pasadena are doing their own work and supplying the transient patronage which is a vital matter for every theater in New York. This art theater is on the whole presenting a higher level of plays than the American stage of 1775 to 1825 did. A reading of a hundred or more of the old classics, and the inevitable comparison with the best that are being produced today, will convince anyone that those products of a courtly tradition were amazing compounds of the sentimental and the utterly unlifelike, only redeemed by occasional ornate or splendid or noble passages, with, in the comedies, rarer bits of sparkling dialogue. The conventional "movie" plot of today is no farther from life than the conventional plot and the basic conceptions of the favorite plays of a hundred years ago. And when it comes to scrupulousness of ensemble acting and studied effects in staging the advantage is overwhelmingly with the present.

These latter claims can be made for the whole stage of today, even the most crassly commercial. Granting that this is in the hands of money-making magnates who will stage any kind of a production that the public will attend and the law will allow, and that in their business tactics they are no more philanthropic than the big dealers in other commodities, the case is not as black as it is often painted. The magnates, whether the dominant middlemen or the producers, are not in a conspiracy to degrade the public taste. They have no more desire to drag it down than they have to lift it up. They are quite willing to stage the world's greatest drama if the public will accord it the world's biggest box office, or even a little less than that. They are in the most uncertain of businesses. If the Shuberts and their compeers could fill their houses from now till doomsday on Sophocles, Shakespeare, Schiller, and Shaw it would be left for free-lance adventurers to risk their money on anything else.

Moreover, the magnates are proceeding on the costly discovery that excellent productions which will pay moderately in New York, with its reputed half-million nightly transients, cannot be made to pay in other cities. This does not prove that the theatrical general headquarters has decreed against letting good plays go out of town; it does not prove that the residents of other cities average lower in dramatic taste than the residents of New York. It proves only that there are more potential playgoers living or visiting in the biggest city in the country than there are in any other. The mention of good drama implies, and rightly, that the commercial theater is not to be absolutely set off from the art theater. It not only often takes its risks on fine plays finely produced, if they seem likely to pay, but it watches the experiments of the art theater, adopts methods of staging, and, for the good of the stage as a whole, hires and richly rewards the men and women in the art theater who have proved they have something fine—which pays. Taking the last eight or ten seasons into the reckoning it is clear that, disregarding the obvious trash, the upper level of plays produced in New York has had more to offer the discriminating playgoer than it offered in the eighteen nineties or in the decade that followed, and that the proportion of such offerings is on the gain rather than on the decline.

The fact that showgoers are in an immense majority over playgoers reveals nothing new and nothing unique about the American public. The commercial theater does not so much pander to the base as cater to the unintelligent. The greatest money-makers of the years will almost invariably include one mercilessly explicit morality play. The prosperity of the commercial theater simply emphasizes one broad and safe conclusion: that in the amusement world the purveyor who consults the public demand will drop toward the level of the bromidic, the stupid, and the obvious. But the rise in importance of the art theater points an equally safe conclusion: that the public will on the whole accept better art than it will demand. The prevalence of the community ventures, the increasing resort to the drama and the theater by schools and colleges, the quickened market for printed plays, are all building up a substantial body of playgoers who as time goes on will increase the support of good plays well acted. Although the showgoers will always vastly predominate in the theatrical world, they are not irrevocably committed to the trivial or the dirty or the goody-goody banal. They are always open to the risk of blundering onto good plays and liking them; they are always open to the possibility of being recruited as at least associate members of the independent order of playgoers. Without them the best of drama would have little chance of stage survival. The American stage, good as well as bad, has more to look for in the support of the showgoer than in the patronage of an eclectic few. It needs and it profits from both. The situation is not one to inspire any patriotic outburst of complacency or gloom. It is one to watch with intensest interest, and it is stimulative of hopes as well as fears.

V

Evidently in thinking of public taste in the United States the distinction should never be lost between the small group whose likings are rooted in consciously recognized tradition and the immense majority who are products of a multitude of traditions and are oblivious of all of them—between the group who hold the attention of Mrs. Wharton, Mr. Hergesheimer, and Mr. Cabell, and the group who represent life to Mr. Dreiser, Mr. Anderson, and Mr. Lewis. The smaller group is obviously of great importance. In a way the aesthetic and intellectual salvation of the country depends upon them. From them comes the support of the university, the art gallery, the best that the theater has to offer, the journals of ideas and opinions, all the best publications. They underwrite the orchestra and the opera. But they represent rather the survival or the espousal of an aristocratic culture than the public taste of a democracy. The great majority flood the colleges, from which they expect either vocational training or some magic veneer of culture, read their own periodicals, maintain the market for the "bestsellers," support the chautauqua, the jazz orchestra, and the "movies." Always the two groups exchange visits and patronage; sometimes they meet on common ground. But they are separate and distinguishable beyond any doubt.

The difference between the two is instanced in the difference between their most distinctive forms of

entertainment: grand opera and the moving picture. It is the difference between the court and the
people, the orchid and the sunflower, patronage and
public support. The programs of the New York and
Chicago opera seasons are practically the same
and completely exotic. The composers are Italian,
French, German, and Russian with an occasional
dubious and short-lived American experiment. The
singers are Italian, French, German, and Russian
with an occasional American who has been taught
to sing in Europe. The conductors—the same. The
personnel of the orchestras—the same. The impres-
sarios, backed by American millions, pay a few of
the soloists fees that soar beyond anything dreamed
of in Europe, and get the money from the millions
partly at exorbitant box prices and partly by hundreds of thousands of underwriting. In the boxes are
the millions, dozily enduring, or the millions'
friends who occasionally relieve them from duty.
In the boxes are also diamonds which are carried for
display into the foyer during the protracted waits
between the acts. The operas themselves, sung un-
intelligibly in foreign tongues, sometimes two or
three in a performance, are marvels of vocalization,
marvels of human co-ordination, marvels of utter
artifice. The only human manifestation to compare
with them are the peacetime field maneuvers of an
army. They are as intricate and wonderful as steel
bridges, suspended in the clouds. There are those
who enjoy them. There are twice or thrice as many

who pretend to enjoy them while enjoying themselves on parade. As no one, or almost no one, is compelled to attend, no one suffers any hardship from their existence. And as the chief underwriters are usually active and open handed in good works it would be churlish to charge them with diverting wealth from legitimate expenditure. But grand opera is as unnecessary to life—even to aesthetic life—as artichokes to public health. And it would languish and die if left to public support.

On the other hand, the financing of the moving picture to the height of its fabulous figures has been secured from this source alone. There are hundreds of moving-picture houses in New York and Chicago. Any one of the largest has as many patrons in the fivefold Sunday overturn as the Metropolitan or Civic Opera has in a week. Each operates fifty-two weeks in the year to the opera's twenty, and it coins money for its owners, though not enough to rival the annual deficit of the operas. It is a new enterprise, working in a gigantic experiment, with mechanical appliances that are every year more effective and mechanical inventors moving so much more rapidly than the artists who should be exploring its possibilities that a theory of moving-picture aesthetics is hardly more than dreamed of. But in the meanwhile the public is ecstatic over the new toy, and paying heavily. It is a fifteen-year-old with a Rolls-Royce. It is enjoying to the limit the power and smoothness of the engine, the luxuriousness of the fittings, and an occasional view. There is so much satisfaction in just sitting in it that one ride is about as welcome as another; so the youngster spends most of his playtime bowling through the finer residence districts or peering over fences surrounding spectacular shows. Once in a while when the ponderous car is turned into a magic carpet and the boy is spirited away to a magic realm, he does not object. He enjoys the best quite as well as the mediocre or the worst. He enjoys the news pictures and enlarges his horizon as he views them. He enjoys the sentimental fictions of a life that is not ideal, but merely false. And he enjoys the release of his imagination into a romantic world of miracles and fantasies and piquant humors just as much, and no more. But as the average man buys his strip tickets for himself and his family he is making possible a cultural experiment the vastest in extent and the fastest in development that civilization has ever known. The strides it has taken in twenty years have been beyond all prophesying. And because the sun shines brightest in California and the promoter moves quickest in America, three-quarters of the world's films are made in America and primarily for American consumption.

In its present phase the moving-picture public is a complete confirmation of the proposition that if asked what they want they will choose the commonplace, but if asked to accept the excellent they will do so with equal readiness. They like the com-

monplace because its commonplaceness is so completely understandable, and they like the excellent
because it exerts a simple human appeal. The greatest moving-picture scenarios are like the greatest
narratives in literature in being enjoyable by the im-
mature mind for a vivid external story and in appeal-
ing to the mature mind by a dozen elements of content and technique that the child does not see and
should not be bothered with. So while the most un-
redeemed banality has its market, the greatest excellence is often the greatest success. And the moving-
picture producer in the midst of a kaleidoscope of
experiment, depending on machine-made plots,
gags, and happy endings, sometimes deviates into
downright splendor, truth and beauty, and carries
the multitude along with him, no more clearly
aware than they are of what has been done or how
it has been achieved.

This generalization is reaffirmed by the music in
the moving-picture palace, the big establishment
more pretentious than the Paris Opera House, with
its orchestra and its organ. The orchestra has fifty
or more members. The organ costs as many thousand dollars. There is a prevailing tradition as to
the kind of music an orchestra shall play. So, while
stopping short of Bach, Brahms, and Beethoven, the
orchestra plays for the most part accepted and acceptable music and plays it very well. That is what
an orchestra is supposed to do, and the people like
it. But the popular tradition of the organ is ob-

viously not to be maintained in the moving-picture theater. It is no place for devotional and religious music. So the chief featuring of the organ is in playing popular "sob" songs as the moonlit or vine-embowered words are thrown on the screen, and playing them with an almost incredible abandonment of sloppy sentimentalism. The public like this just as much as they do the orchestra.

The most ingenious recognition of this double trait of the miscellaneous audience is the makeup and presentation of a Paul Whiteman concert program. Mr. Whiteman has an accomplishment and an ideal of art. He sees the one and never forgets the other, and combines the two in such a way as to keep the people swarming to his concerts. The program as announced and presented is musically ambitious—symphonies, tone-poems, suites, with a little interpolated concert encore music; and it is played seriously and excellently. Vast audiences listen to this, which is what he wants to play. It is interesting and on the way to something; and it is soon over —in an hour to an hour and a quarter. Then when Whiteman the musician has had his way, Whiteman the showman takes the stage in a long series of unannounced but evidently programmed afterpieces. He plays jazz that has gone into recent records, introduces "the boys" under the spotlight on a darkened stage as one after another displays his extraordinary proficiency; he injects straight comedy "stunts" : a monologue man, a trick fiddler who

also plays a duet on two wind instruments and a
solo on a bicycle pump. By the time the first violin-
ist has performed on the harmonica, the second
has burst out in a *tenore robusto*, the cornetist has
squawked, and the soprano saxophonist has twit-
tered, the audience are in an uproar of enthusiasm.
It all flows along very casually, but it is all carefully
planned. At the end of two hours the "encores" are
over. The audience go home feeling that they have
had more than they bargained for and eager to come
again, and Whiteman, the astute, has had the
double satisfaction of playing what he wanted, giving the public what they wanted, and making them
enjoy both and ask for more.

VI

Flouting of adult education in the United States
is still indulged in by certain of the fastidious and
uninformed, though it ought long ago to have
ceased even in the gang talk of the intelligentsia. It
is continued with various degrees of undiscrimina-
tion by those who are indifferent or hostile to any
bridging of the gap between the creative artist, the
scientist, the scholar, the critic, and the totally ignorant; and for purposes of comfortable classifica-
tion the flouters are ready to group together the il-
literate, the public-school product, most collegians,
the average clergyman, the village doctor, all con-
gressmen and their wives. It is the wives who cause
most discomfort to the skeptics because they display

the most active stirrings of curiosity. They are terrible organizers; "they pursue Culture in bands, as though it were dangerous to meet alone." Not content with dabbling with political and social reforms they invade the domains of art, literature, and travel. While with the right hand they are closing the saloon and ringing the curfew, with the left they are sending out invitations to "view days" at the art gallery, to subscription concerts, to lyceum courses, to Drama League performances, to chautauquas, to open, and general, and departmental, and board, and committee meetings of their clubs. They are feminizing culture; which, say the flouters, is ridiculous because they can't tell a masterpiece from a chromo, a poem from the worst of doggerel, good music from slop, an idea from a hole in the ground.

The flouters never take the pains to offer substitutes for the activities they hold in such contempt. They would not improve the woman's club and the chautauqua; they would not replace them. They would simply blast them with a few epigrams and stop at that—which is quite obviously more ridiculous than the proceedings of the flouted. For they, when the worst is said of them, are better occupied in spite of every epigram than if they were ignoring the arts and literatures and travels and ideas of which they are trying to achieve some grasp. The point would not be worth dwelling on if it were not for the prevalence of cheaply derogatory talk. The aesthetes and intelligents who allege so much about life are always giving away their ignorance of it when they display their contempt for the average commoner. On the side of learning they sneer at all the unlearned who would like to know a little more. They have no patience with any who cannot read Greek drama in the original—one out of every hundred, if the truth be known, of those who have "taken" Greek, ninety-nine of whom had such light cases that it has only served as an inoculant. Unless the modern reader can enjoy Aeschylus with intimate knowledge and delight he must forego the translations of Sir Gilbert Murray, which of course he does not need. On the side of art they pour out the little vials of their contempt on all who cannot feel every nuance that they themselves can in the art museum or the orchestra hall.

There is a pleasant irony in the fact that the most insistently scornful talkers about the "bourgeoisie" in America—a group who speak as evangels of modernism, emancipators from the trammels of the past—in freeing themselves from Victorianism, the code of the nineteenth century in England, and from Puritanism, the code of the seventeenth century in New England, have only returned to the English code of the eighteenth century, the code prevailing from Swift and Pope to Churchill and Gifford and Byron. And, although none but Mr. Cabell seems to be clear as to his genealogy, there is a reason. For at many points the America of today is like the England of two centuries ago. There is the same prevailing assault on dulness and on sentimentalism because the demagogue and the evangelist are high in public esteem. The people are asserting themselves now as they were then. What the revolutions of the late eighteenth century started the world-confusion of the twentieth century is following up. The dulness and sentimentalism of the former day bore fruit in a fresh reassertion of the human spirit, led to fresh and vital art in many forms, and developed a public to replace the patron and a citizenry to replace a yokelry.

So far the parallel is a fair one; but though history parallels itself it does not repeat itself. The ultra-moderns, many of whom are acutely aware of the facts of the day, still talk as though from an eighteenth-century rostrum. They tell you that America is not English, which is measurably true, but speak from the assumption that a mistaken quantity in a Latin quotation should discredit a congressional orator. They tell you that the past is a sink of erroneous prejudices, and lament that the culture of America falls short of the culture of Europe which is built upon that past.

The sum of the matter seems to be—so far as such a matter can be summarized—that the likeness to the later eighteenth century is somewhat more suggestive than the differences. Certain fine traditions are surviving, and the public is not oblivious to them; but a new public is developing with the beginnings of a taste of its own, with an enormous educational procedure that is in some small degree at least heightening its powers of appreciation, and with mechanical devices which bring to eye and ear sights and sounds for better and for worse. It is through the impressions that are less consciously received that preferences and tastes are most enduringly formed. On the other hand, in cultural experience it is not impossible by taking thought to add, if not a cubit, some slight increase to one's stature; and much of the public is taking thought in this expectation.

There is all the room that the most confirmed Jeremiah could desire for devastating talk and lugubrious prophecy. There is little chance for the operations of any cultural messiah. What happens will happen slowly as the social and material life of America evolves. But there is room for an Abraham, too. Throughout his speeches and writings Lincoln inclined to the conclusion that in human affairs there were always the opinion of the many and the opinion of the few, and that in immediate judgments the opinion of the few was more to be trusted, though in time the opinion of the many not infrequently came round to it. Lincoln was in a broad sense speaking then about democracy and public taste. He was not without hope for the public. Nor do I, in the face of what can be known from the last hundred and fifty years, see any sound reason for disagreeing with him.

Index

Index

PRINTED
IN U·S·A·